W9-BFU-639

THE BATTLE OF THE ALAMO

written and illustrated by
Rod Espinosa

visit us at
www.abdopublishing.com

Published by Red Wagon, a division of the ABDO Publishing Group, 8000 West 78th Street, Edina, Minnesota 55439. Copyright © 2008 by Abdo Consulting Group, Inc. International copyrights reserved in all countries. All rights reserved. No part of this book may be reproduced in any form without written permission from the publisher. Graphic Planet™ is a trademark and logo of Red Wagon.

Printed in the United States.

Written and illustrated by Rod Espinosa
Colored and lettered by Rod Espinosa
Edited by Stephanie Hedlund
Interior layout and design by Antarctic Press
Cover art by Brian Dehnam and GURU-eFX
Cover design by Neil Klinepier

Library of Congress Cataloging-in-Publication Data

Espinosa, Rod.
    The Battle of the Alamo / Rod Espinosa.
    p. cm. -- (Graphic history)
    Includes index.
    ISBN 978-1-60270-073-4
    1. Alamo (San Antonio, Tex.)--Siege, 1836--Juvenile literature. 2. Graphic novels. I. Title.

F390.E88 2008
741.5358--dc22

2007004342

TABLE of CONTENTS

Chapter 1
Defending the Alamo.............................4

Chapter 2
The Mexicans Arrive.............................10

Chapter 3
The Siege Begins.............................15

Chapter 4
The Line in the Sand.............................20

Chapter 5
The Battle of the Alamo.............................22

Chapter 6
The Fall of the Alamo.............................24

Map of the Alamo.............................28

Timeline.............................30

Glossary.............................31

Web Sites.............................31

Index.............................32

Chapter 1 Defending the Alamo

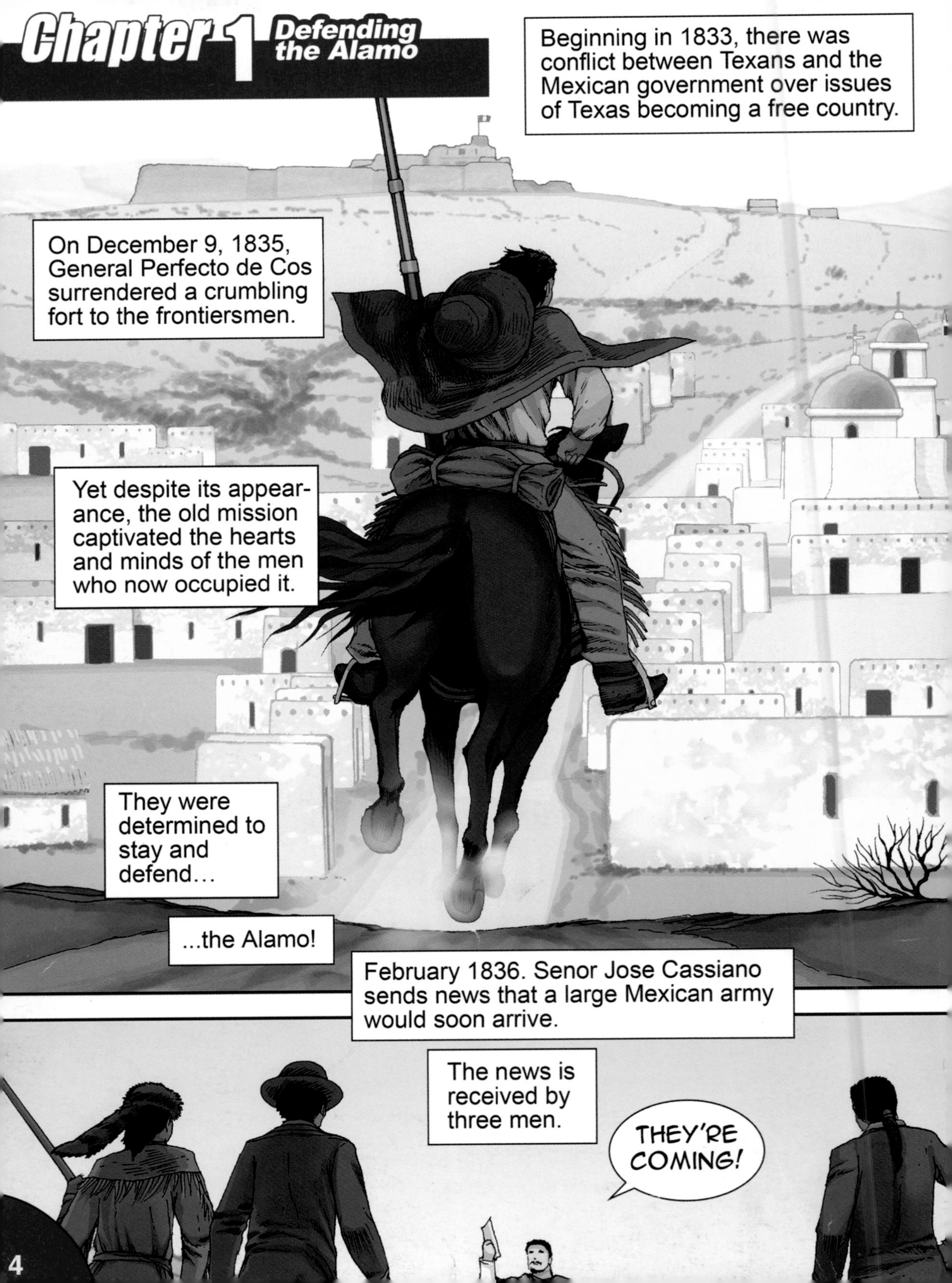

Beginning in 1833, there was conflict between Texans and the Mexican government over issues of Texas becoming a free country.
On December 9, 1835, General Perfecto de Cos surrendered a crumbling fort to the frontiersmen.
Yet despite its appearance, the old mission captivated the hearts and minds of the men who now occupied it.
They were determined to stay and defend…
...the Alamo!
February 1836. Senor Jose Cassiano sends news that a large Mexican army would soon arrive.
The news is received by three men.
THEY'RE COMING!

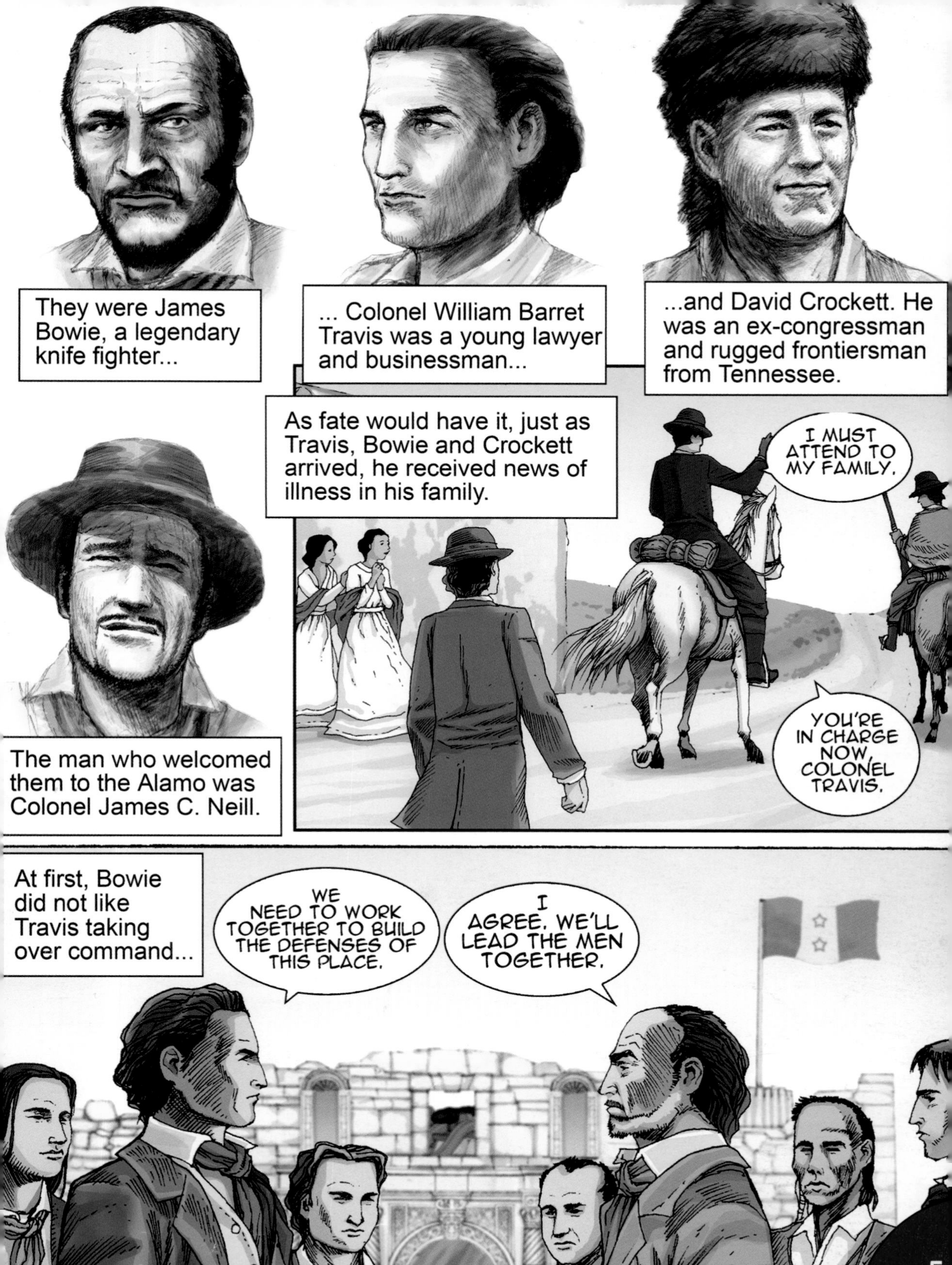

They were James Bowie, a legendary knife fighter...
... Colonel William Barret Travis was a young lawyer and businessman...
...and David Crockett. He was an ex-congressman and rugged frontiersman from Tennessee.
The man who welcomed them to the Alamo was Colonel James C. Neill.
As fate would have it, just as Travis, Bowie and Crockett arrived, he received news of illness in his family.
I MUST ATTEND TO MY FAMILY.
YOU'RE IN CHARGE NOW, COLONEL TRAVIS.
At first, Bowie did not like Travis taking over command...
WE NEED TO WORK TOGETHER TO BUILD THE DEFENSES OF THIS PLACE.
I AGREE. WE'LL LEAD THE MEN TOGETHER.

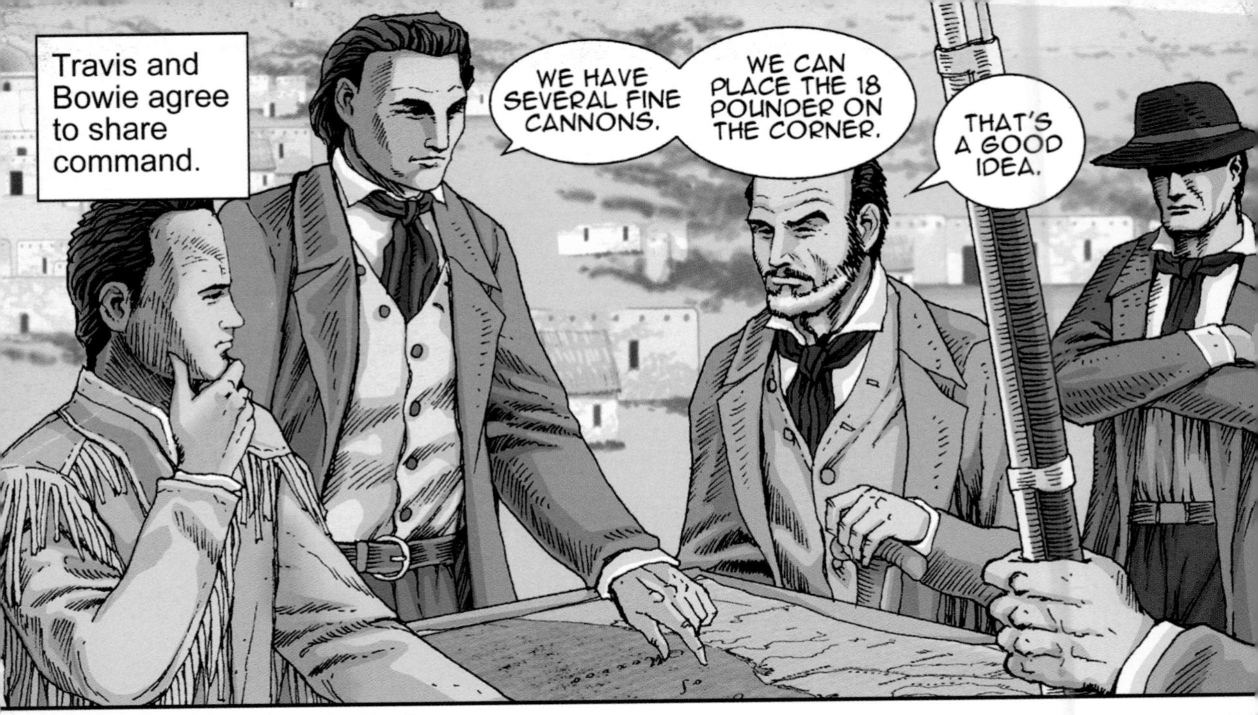
Travis and Bowie agree to share command.
WE HAVE SEVERAL FINE CANNONS.
WE CAN PLACE THE 18 POUNDER ON THE CORNER.
THAT'S A GOOD IDEA.

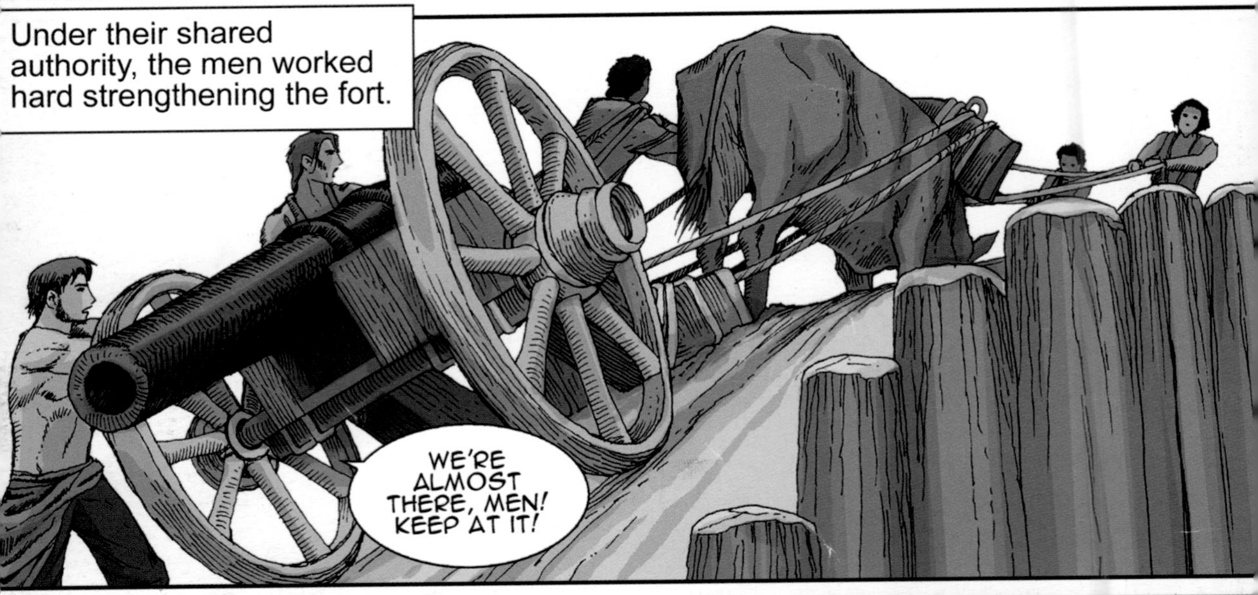
Under their shared authority, the men worked hard strengthening the fort.
WE'RE ALMOST THERE, MEN! KEEP AT IT!

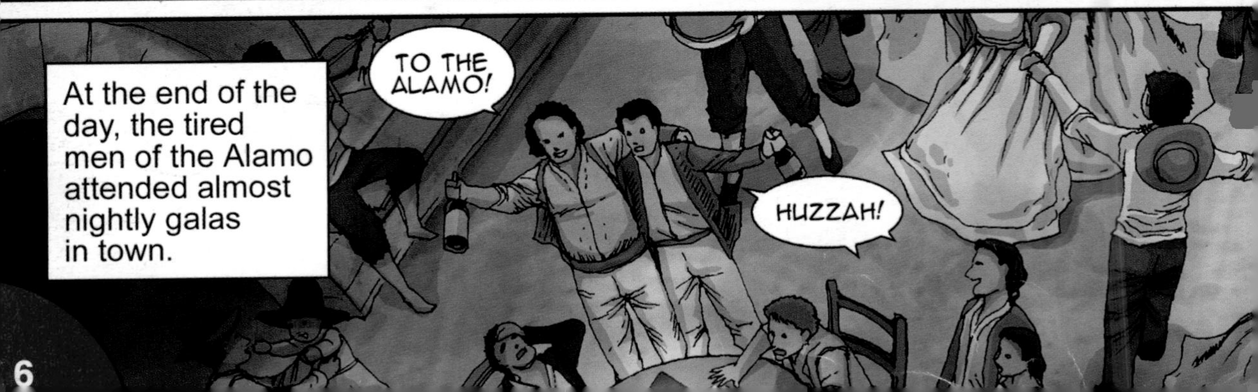
At the end of the day, the tired men of the Alamo attended almost nightly galas in town.
TO THE ALAMO!
HUZZAH!

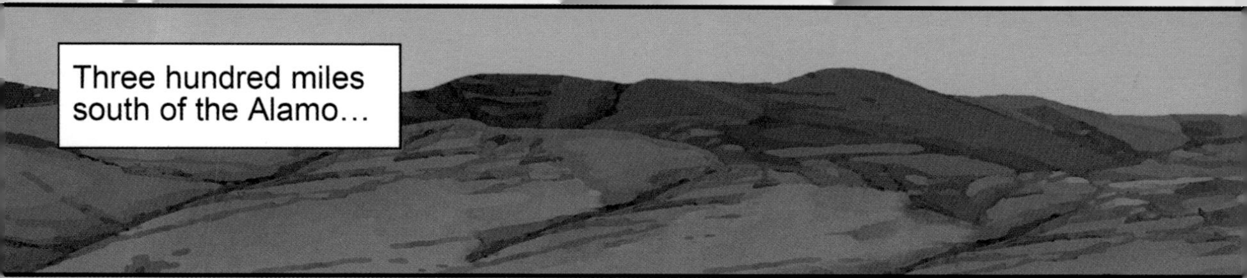
Three hundred miles
south of the Alamo…

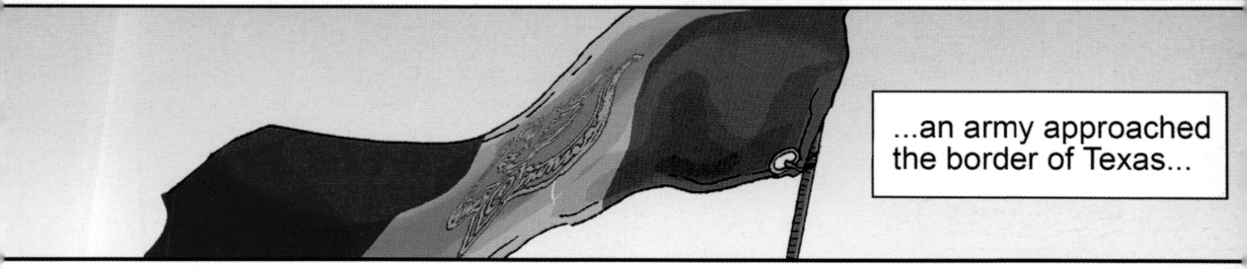
...an army approached
the border of Texas...

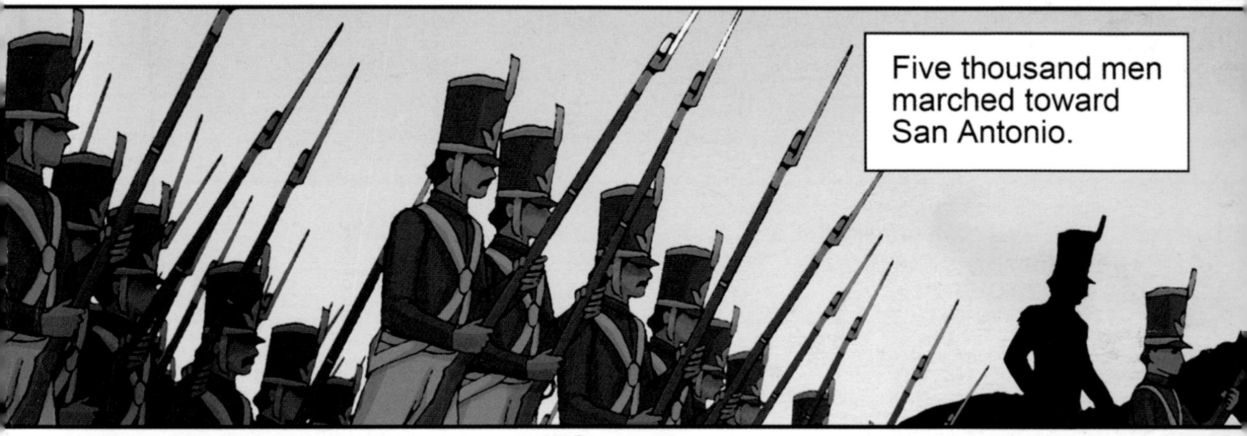
Five thousand men
marched toward
San Antonio.

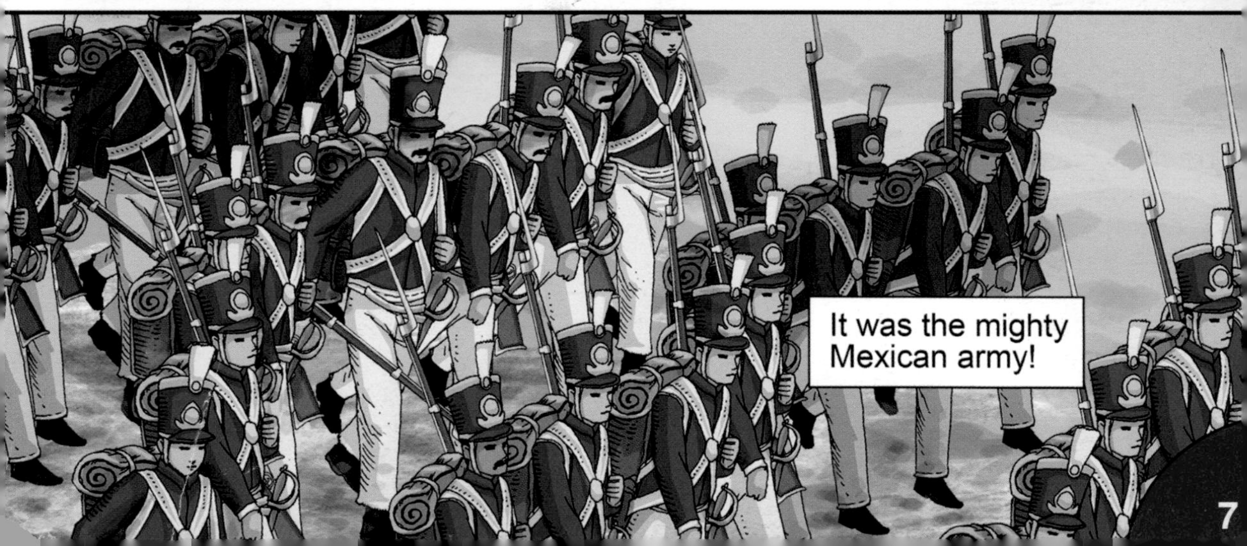
It was the mighty
Mexican army!

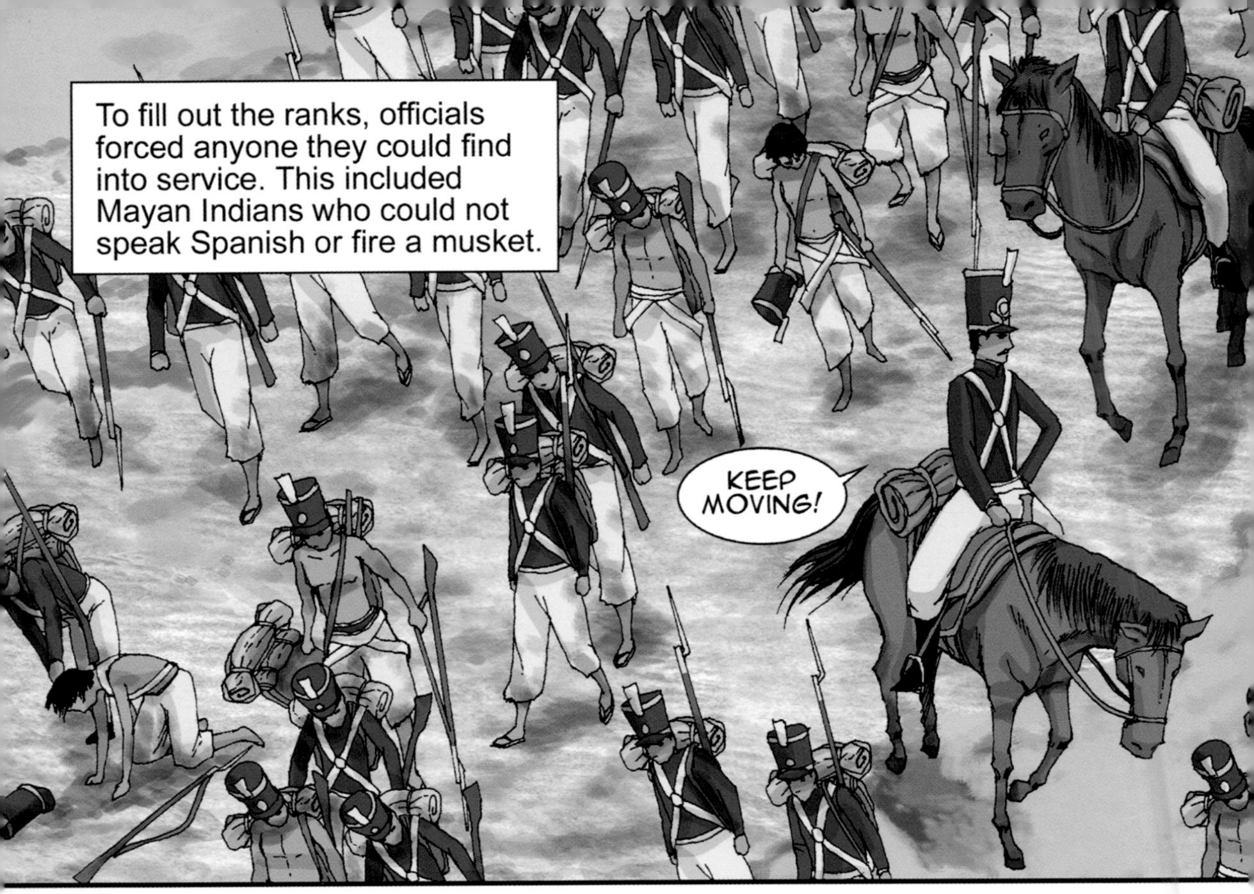
To fill out the ranks, officials forced anyone they could find into service. This included Mayan Indians who could not speak Spanish or fire a musket.
KEEP MOVING!

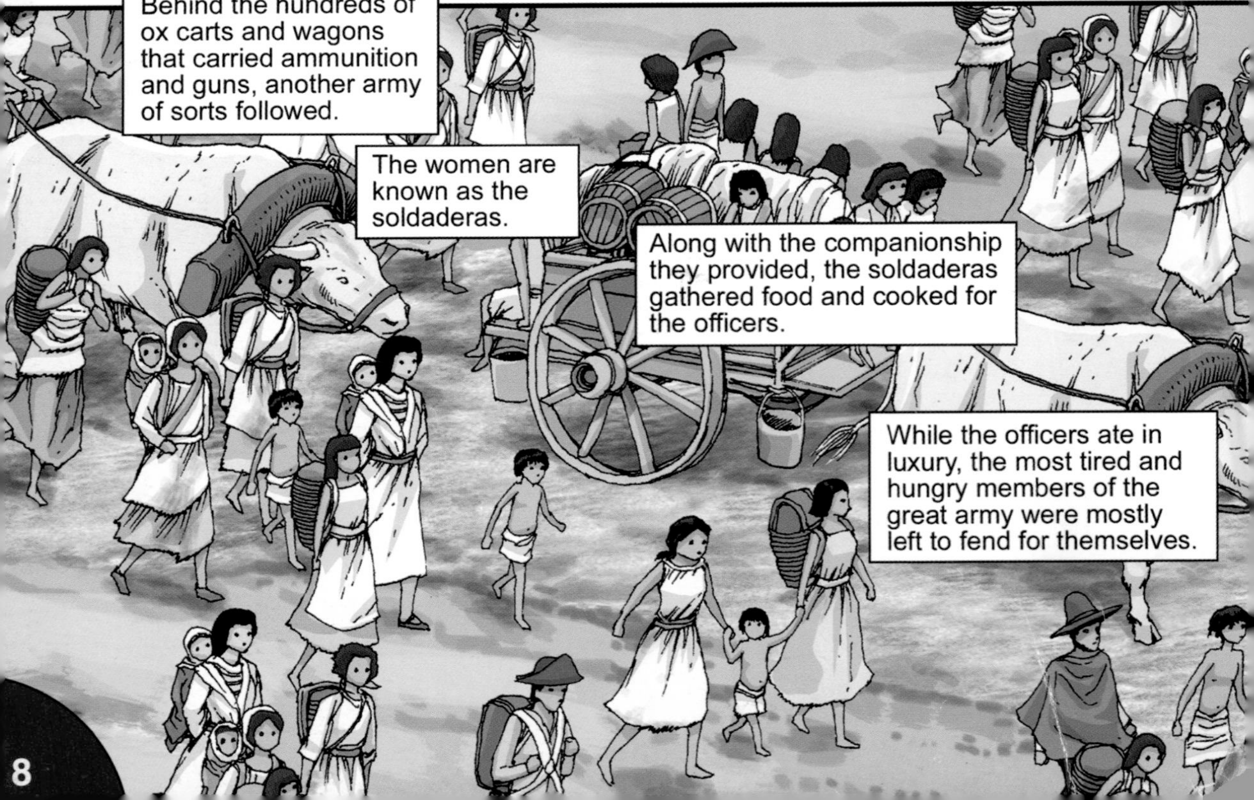
Behind the hundreds of ox carts and wagons that carried ammunition and guns, another army of sorts followed.
The women are known as the soldaderas.
Along with the companionship they provided, the soldaderas gathered food and cooked for the officers.
While the officers ate in luxury, the most tired and hungry members of the great army were mostly left to fend for themselves.

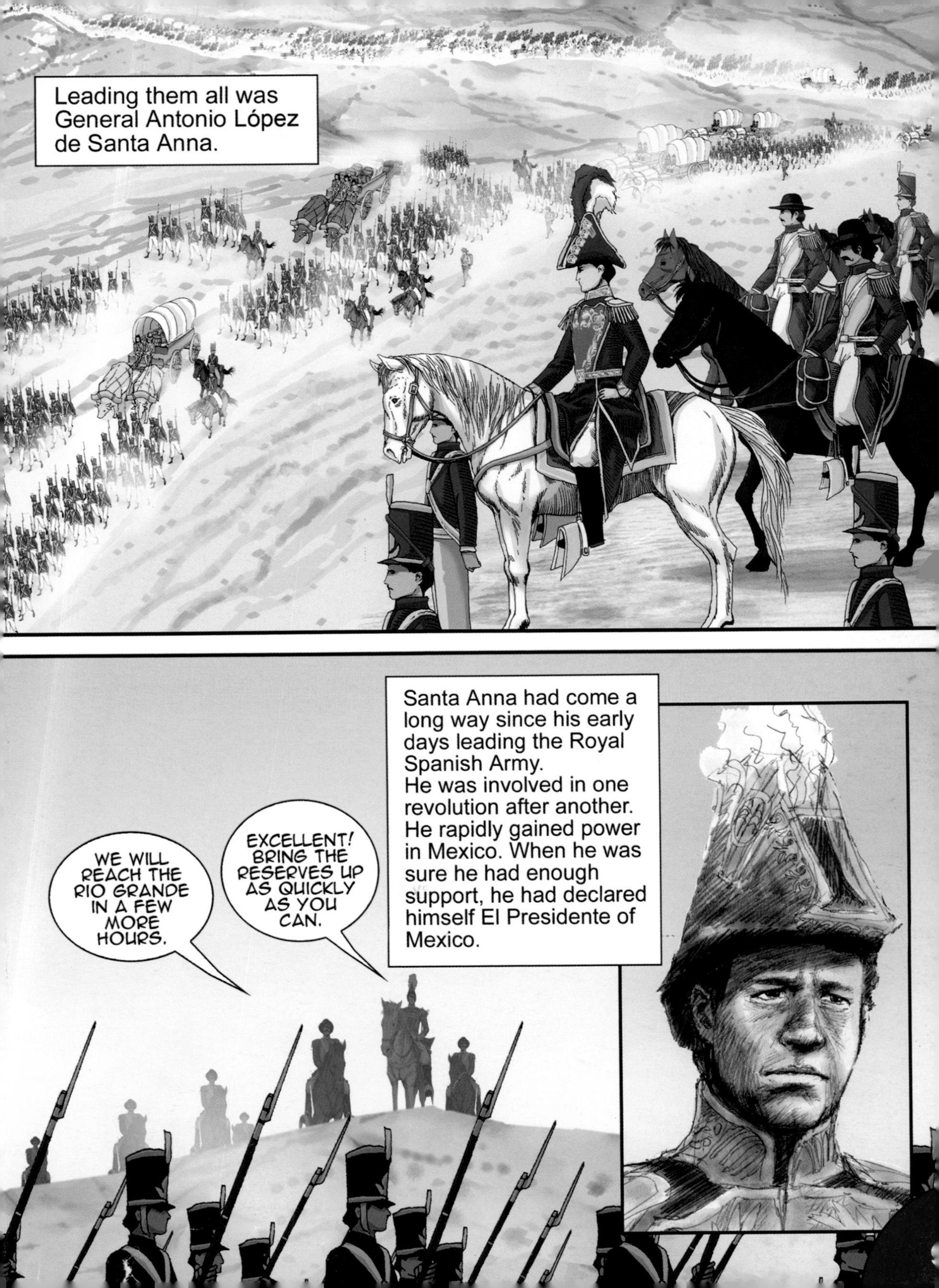

Leading them all was General Antonio López de Santa Anna.
Santa Anna had come a long way since his early days leading the Royal Spanish Army.
He was involved in one revolution after another.
He rapidly gained power in Mexico. When he was sure he had enough support, he had declared himself El Presidente of Mexico.
WE WILL REACH THE RIO GRANDE IN A FEW MORE HOURS.
EXCELLENT! BRING THE RESERVES UP AS QUICKLY AS YOU CAN.

Chapter 2 The Mexicans Arrive

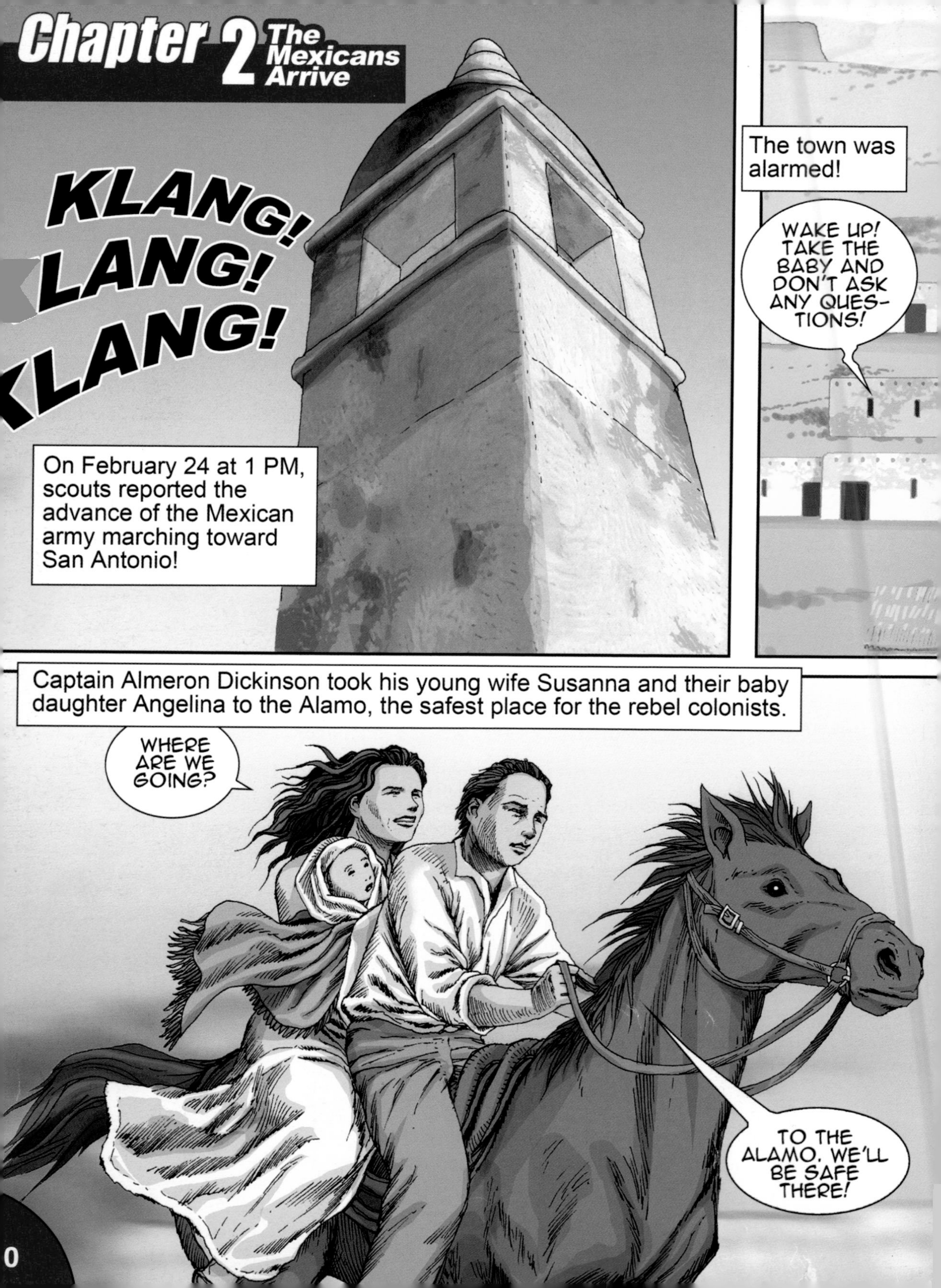
KLANG!
LANG!
KLANG!
On February 24 at 1 PM, scouts reported the advance of the Mexican army marching toward San Antonio!
The town was alarmed!
WAKE UP! TAKE THE BABY AND DON'T ASK ANY QUES-TIONS!
Captain Almeron Dickinson took his young wife Susanna and their baby daughter Angelina to the Alamo, the safest place for the rebel colonists.
WHERE ARE WE GOING?
TO THE ALAMO. WE'LL BE SAFE THERE!

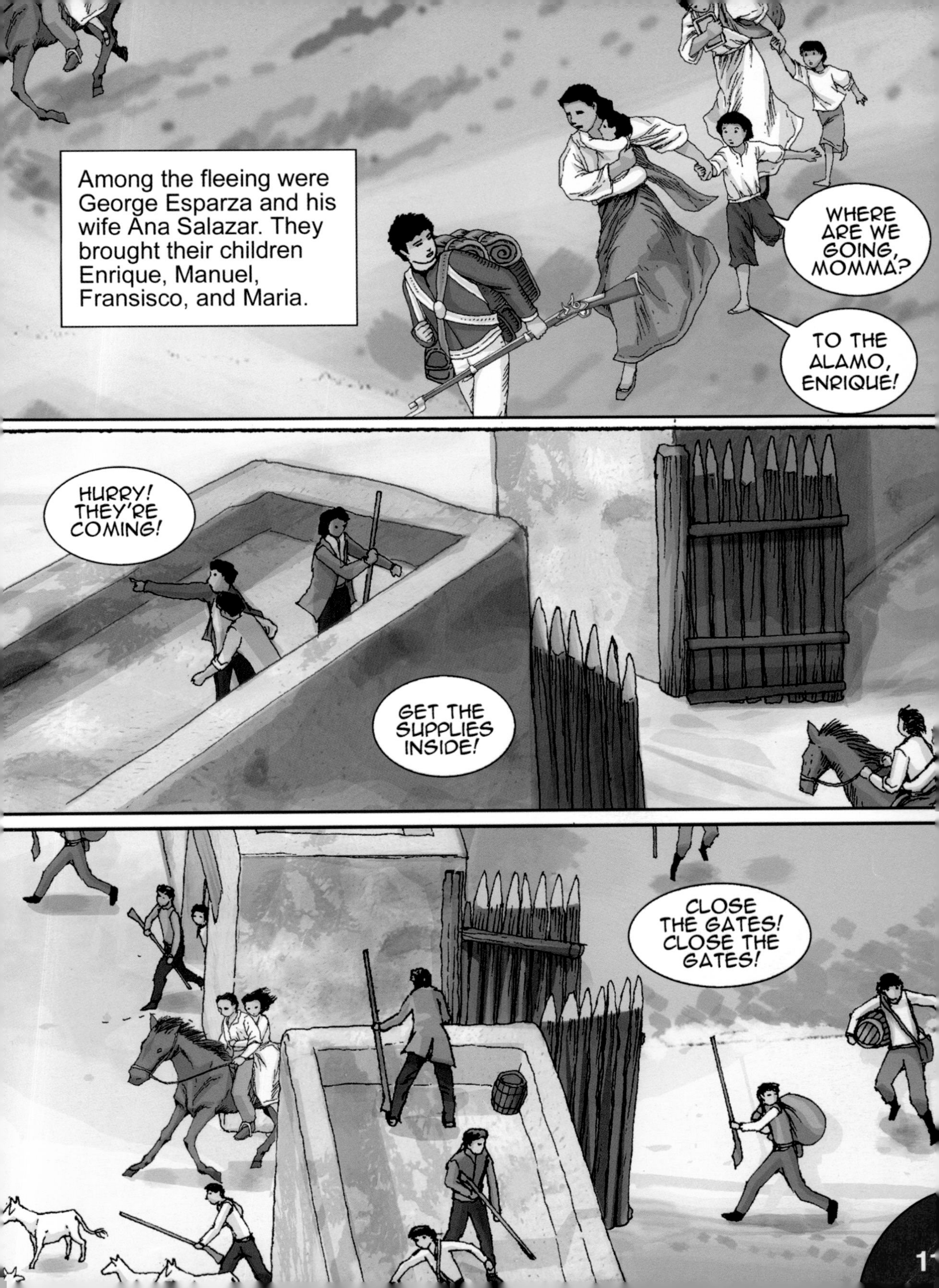
Among the fleeing were George Esparza and his wife Ana Salazar. They brought their children Enrique, Manuel, Fransisco, and Maria.
WHERE ARE WE GOING, MOMMA?
TO THE ALAMO, ENRIQUE!
HURRY! THEY'RE COMING!
GET THE SUPPLIES INSIDE!
CLOSE THE GATES! CLOSE THE GATES!

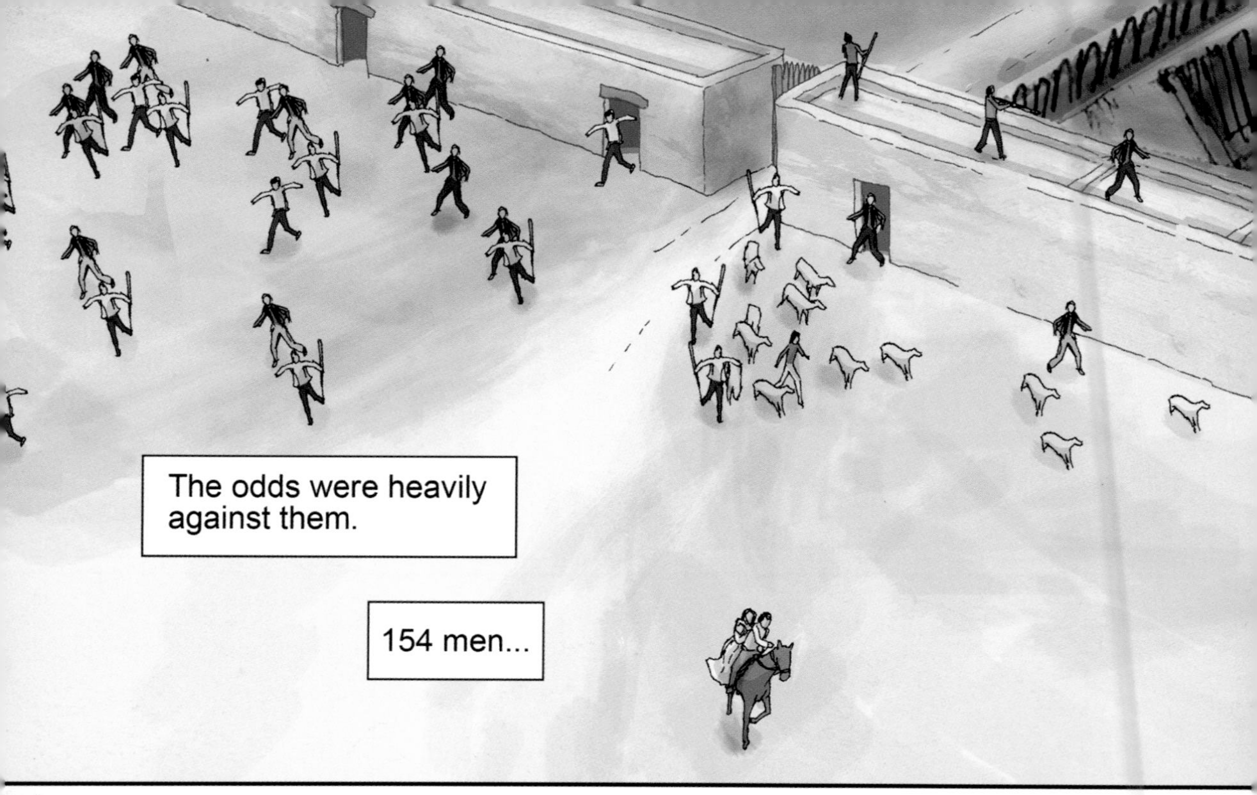
The odds were heavily against them.
154 men...

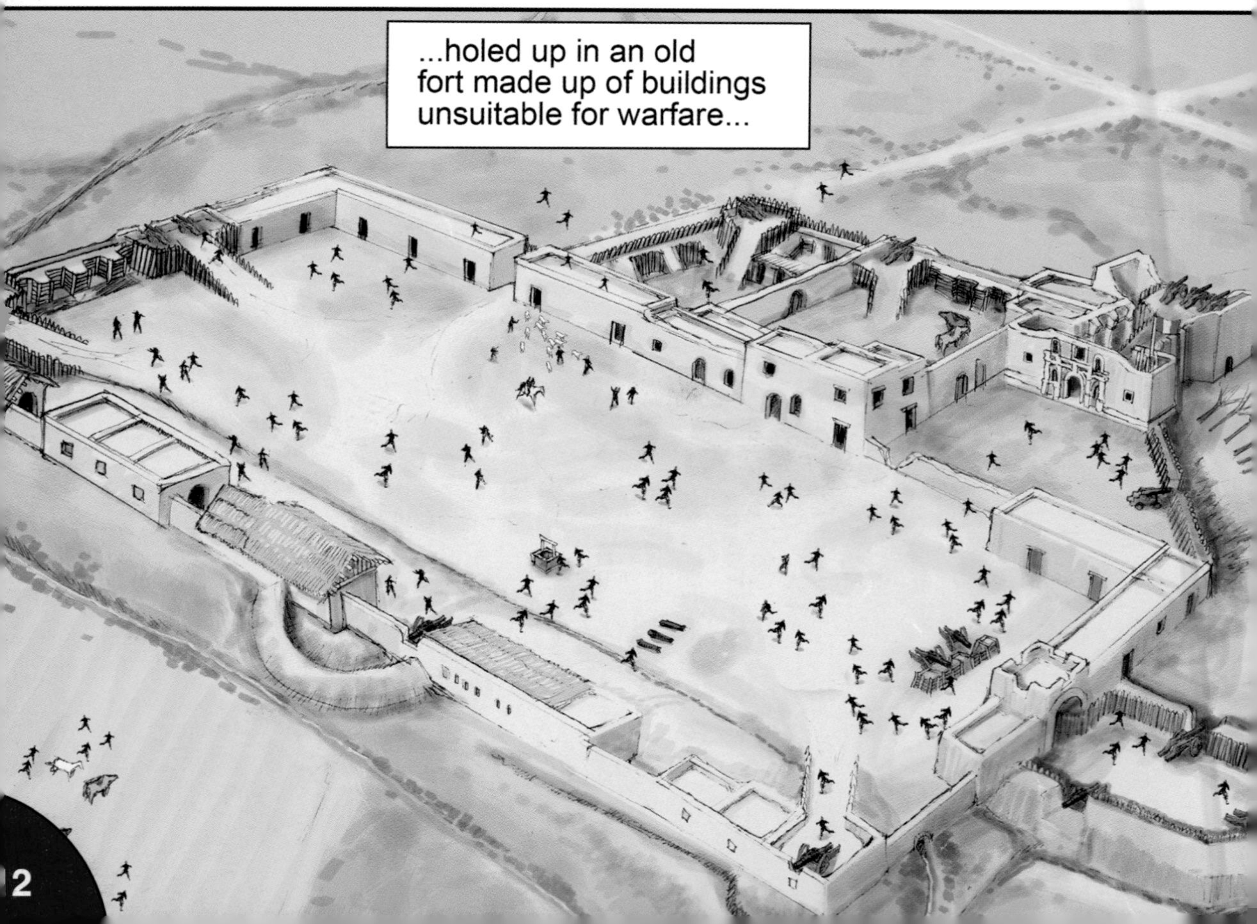
...holed up in an old fort made up of buildings unsuitable for warfare...

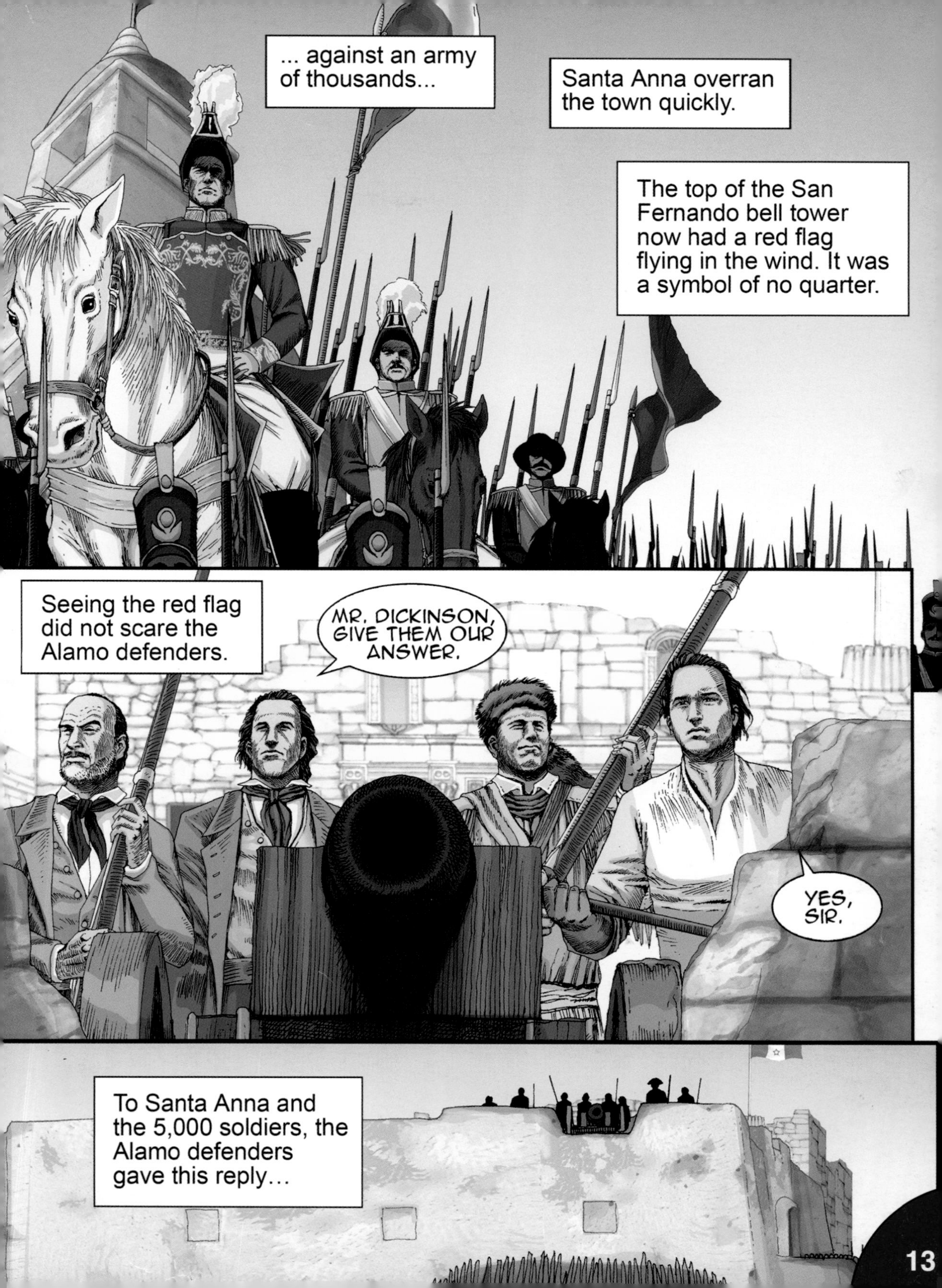
... against an army of thousands...
Santa Anna overran the town quickly.
The top of the San Fernando bell tower now had a red flag flying in the wind. It was a symbol of no quarter.
Seeing the red flag did not scare the Alamo defenders.
MR. DICKINSON, GIVE THEM OUR ANSWER.
YES, SIR.
To Santa Anna and the 5,000 soldiers, the Alamo defenders gave this reply...

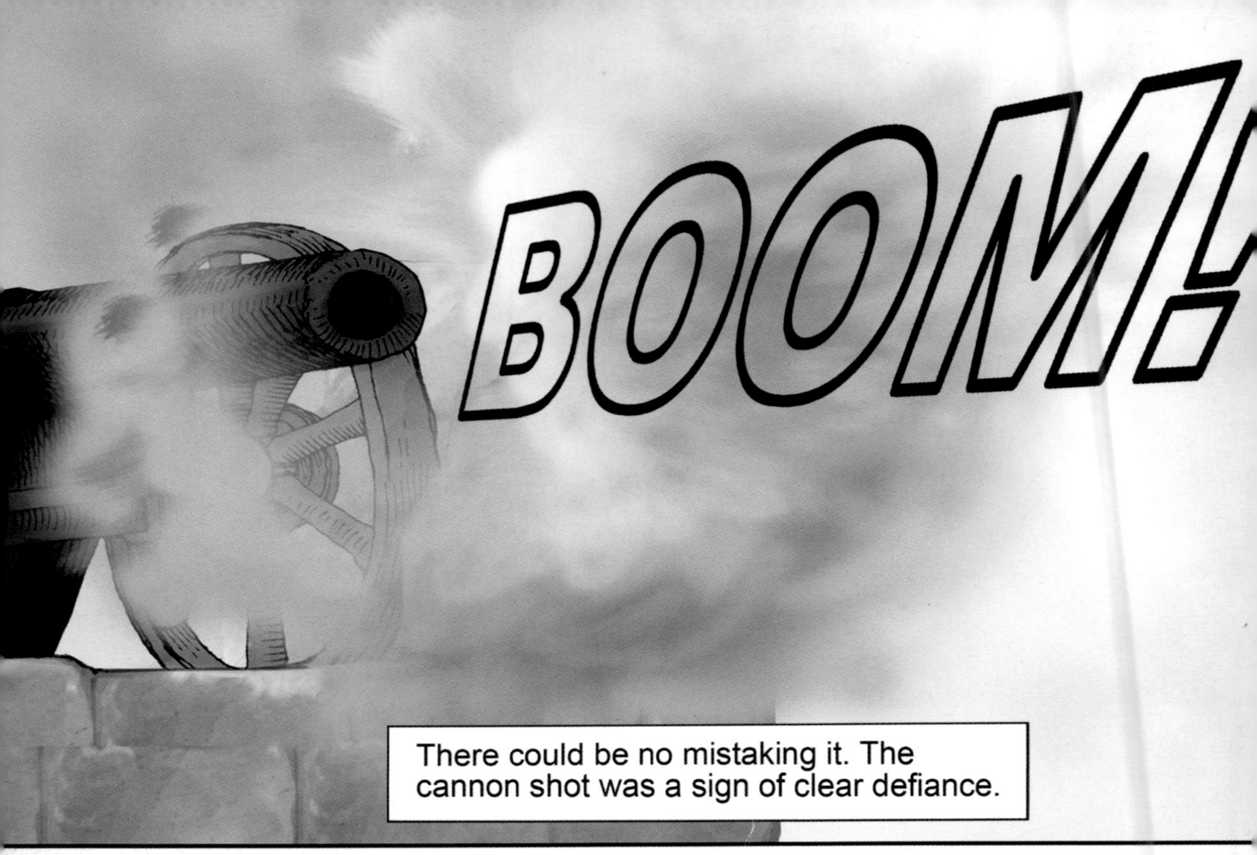
BOOM!
There could be no mistaking it. The cannon shot was a sign of clear defiance.

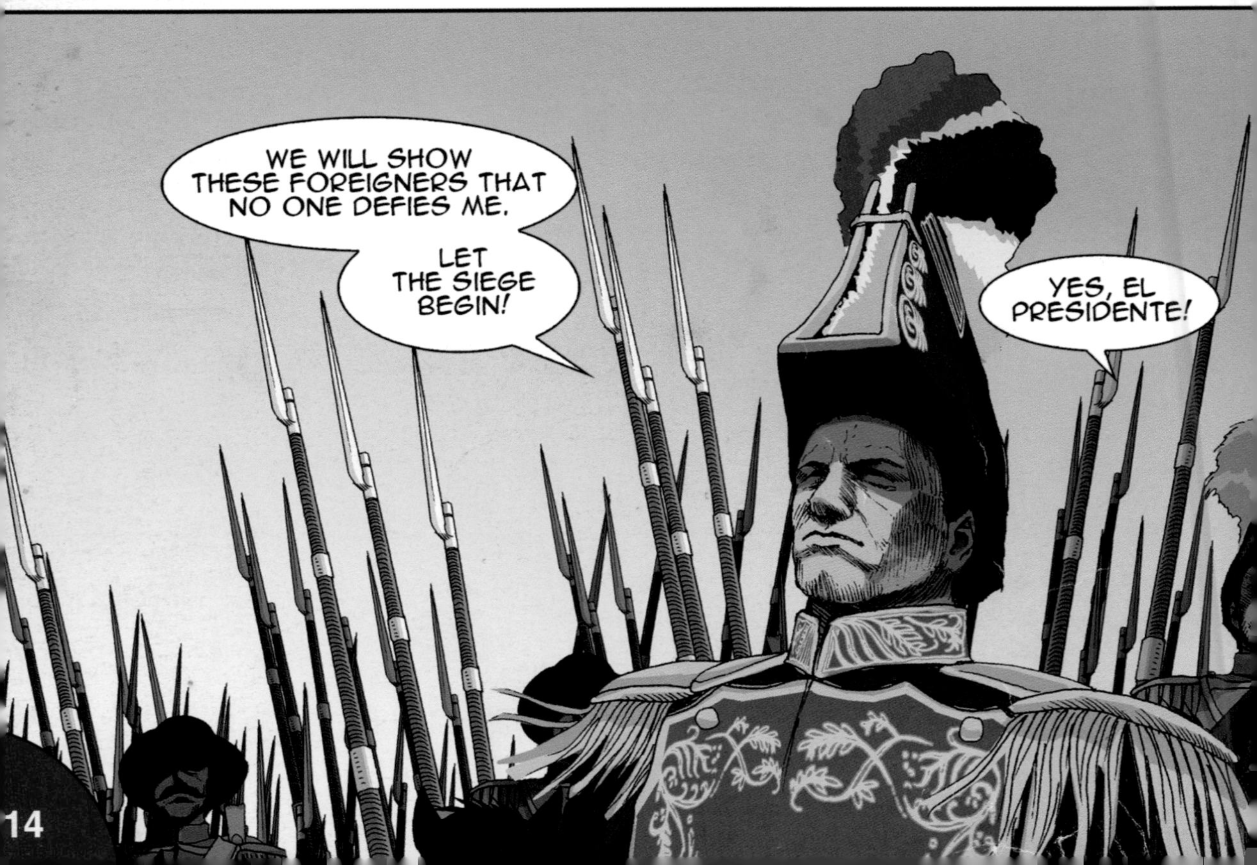
WE WILL SHOW THESE FOREIGNERS THAT NO ONE DEFIES ME.
LET THE SIEGE BEGIN!
YES, EL PRESIDENTE!

Chapter 3 The Siege Begins

Santa Anna had been educated in Europe in the art of siege warfare. He ordered a series of artillery emplacements dug all around the Alamo.

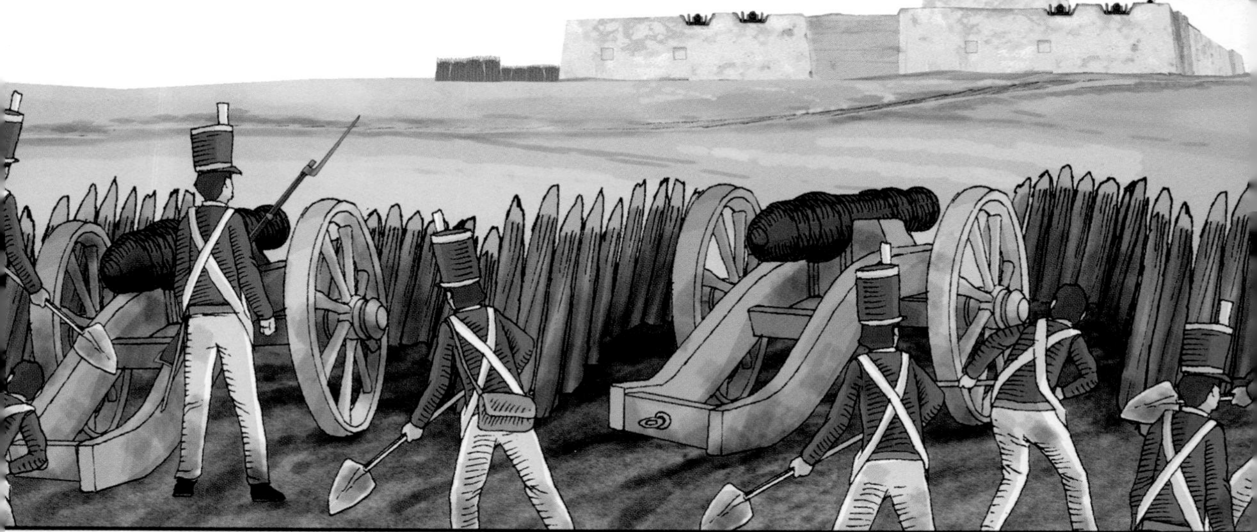

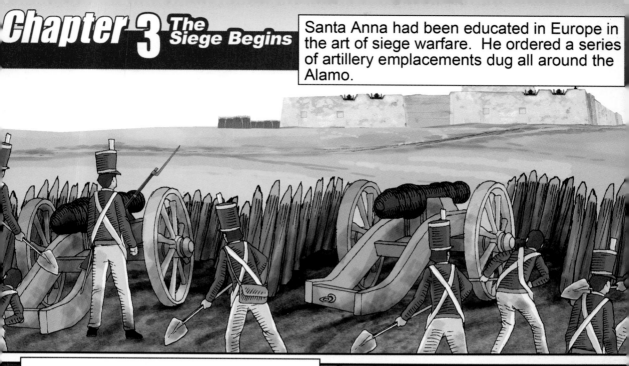

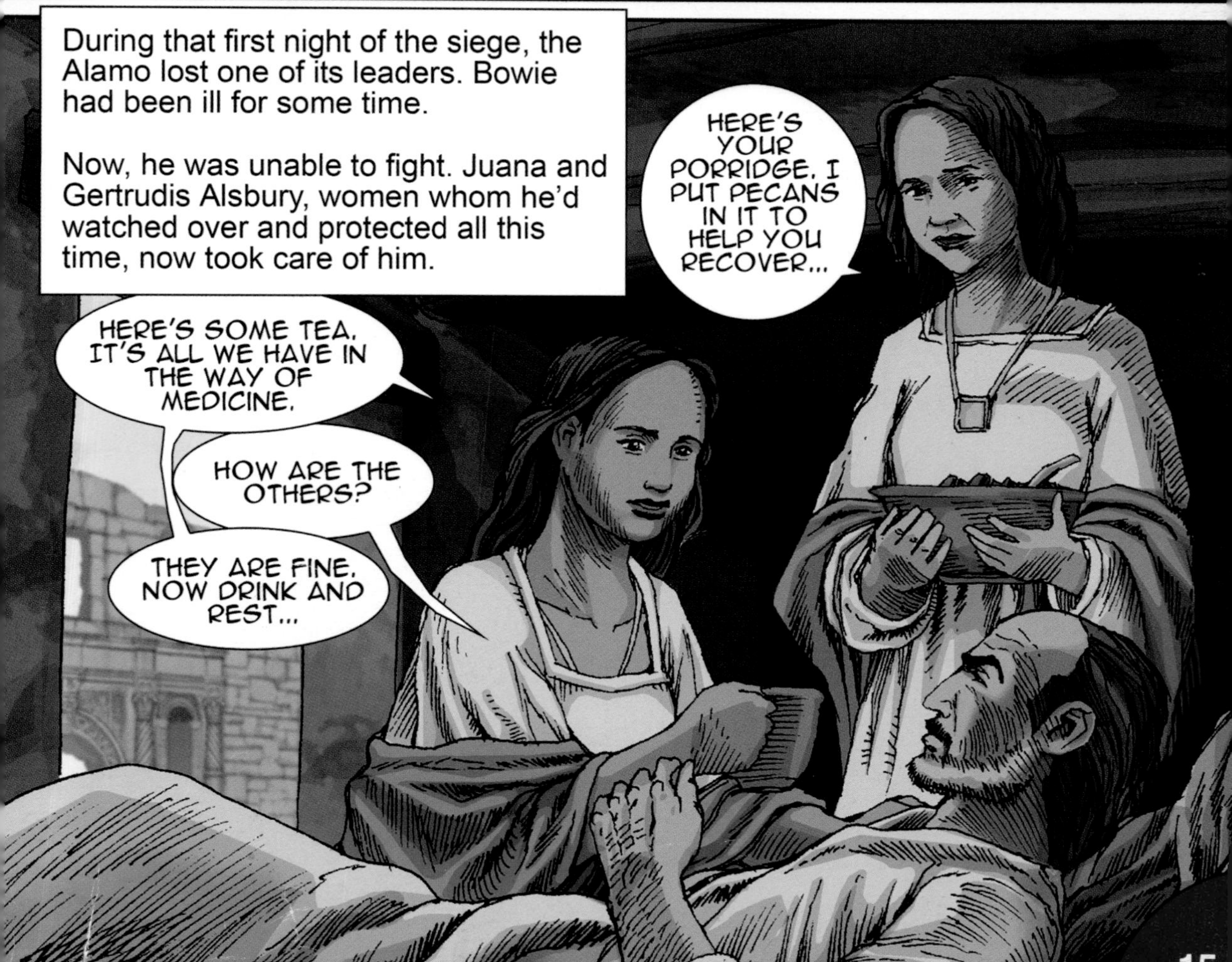
During that first night of the siege, the Alamo lost one of its leaders. Bowie had been ill for some time.
Now, he was unable to fight. Juana and Gertrudis Alsbury, women whom he'd watched over and protected all this time, now took care of him.
HERE'S YOUR PORRIDGE. I PUT PECANS IN IT TO HELP YOU RECOVER...
HERE'S SOME TEA. IT'S ALL WE HAVE IN THE WAY OF MEDICINE.
HOW ARE THE OTHERS?
THEY ARE FINE. NOW DRINK AND REST...

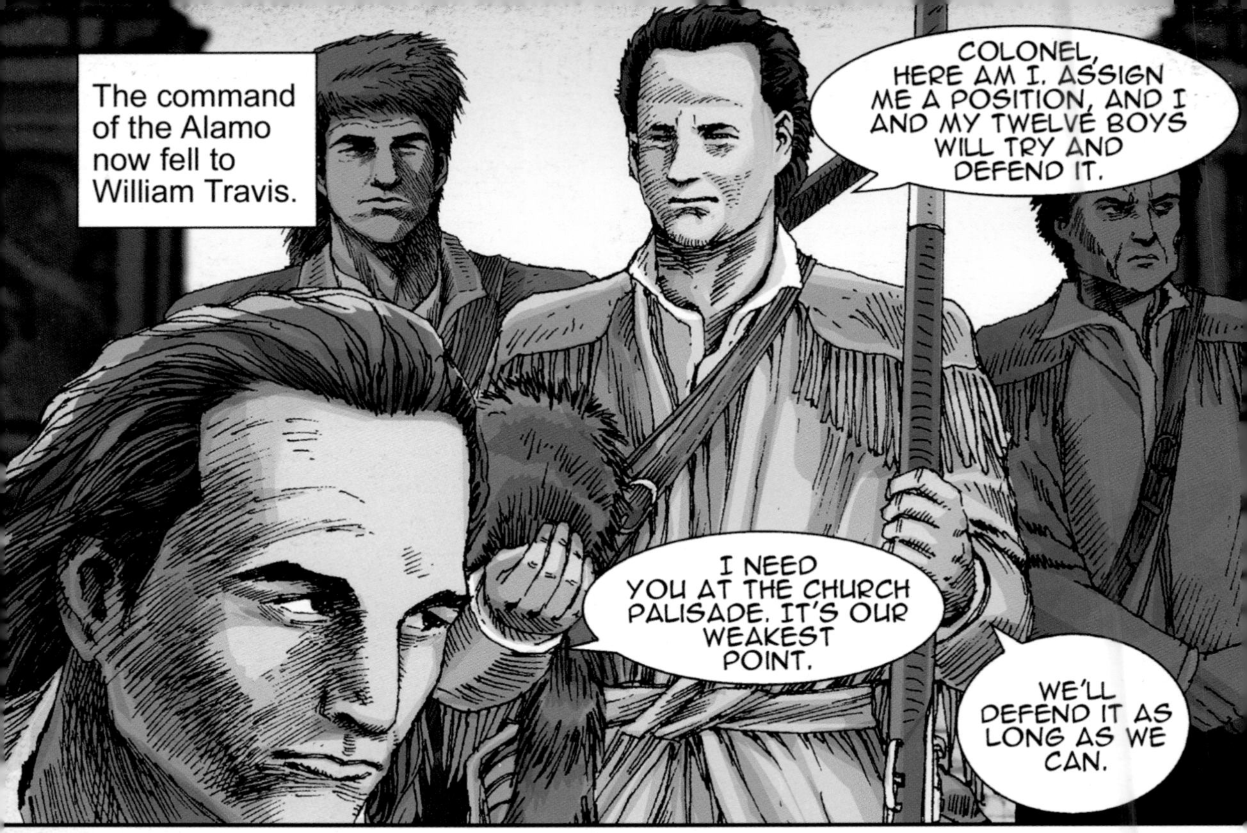
The command of the Alamo now fell to William Travis.
COLONEL, HERE AM I. ASSIGN ME A POSITION, AND I AND MY TWELVE BOYS WILL TRY AND DEFEND IT.
I NEED YOU AT THE CHURCH PALISADE. IT'S OUR WEAKEST POINT.
WE'LL DEFEND IT AS LONG AS WE CAN.

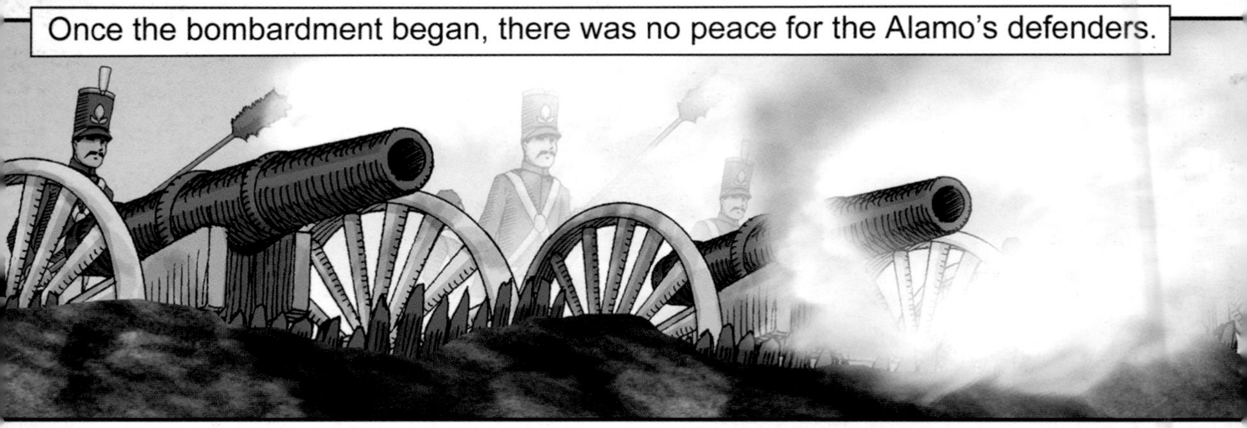
Once the bombardment began, there was no peace for the Alamo's defenders.

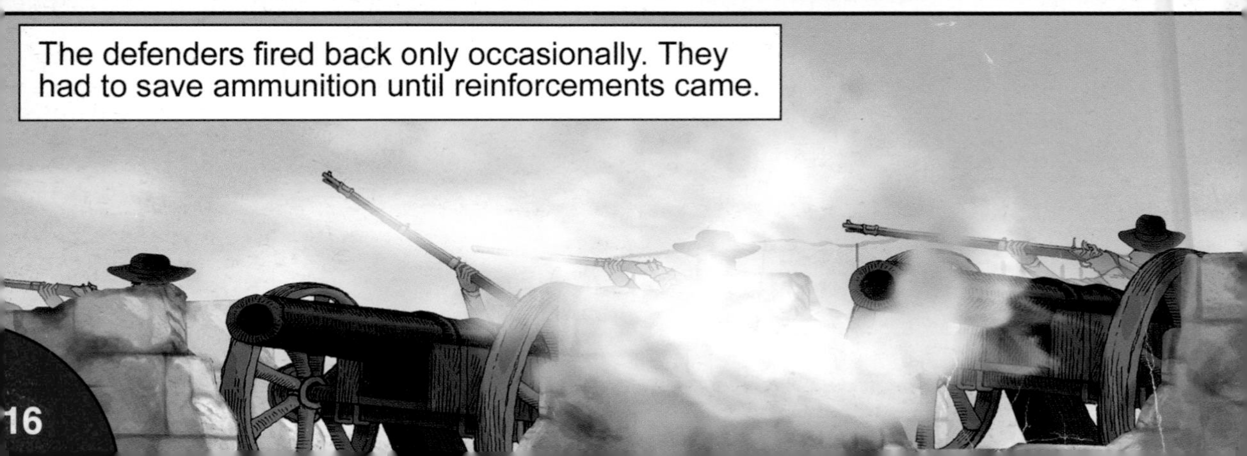
The defenders fired back only occasionally. They had to save ammunition until reinforcements came.

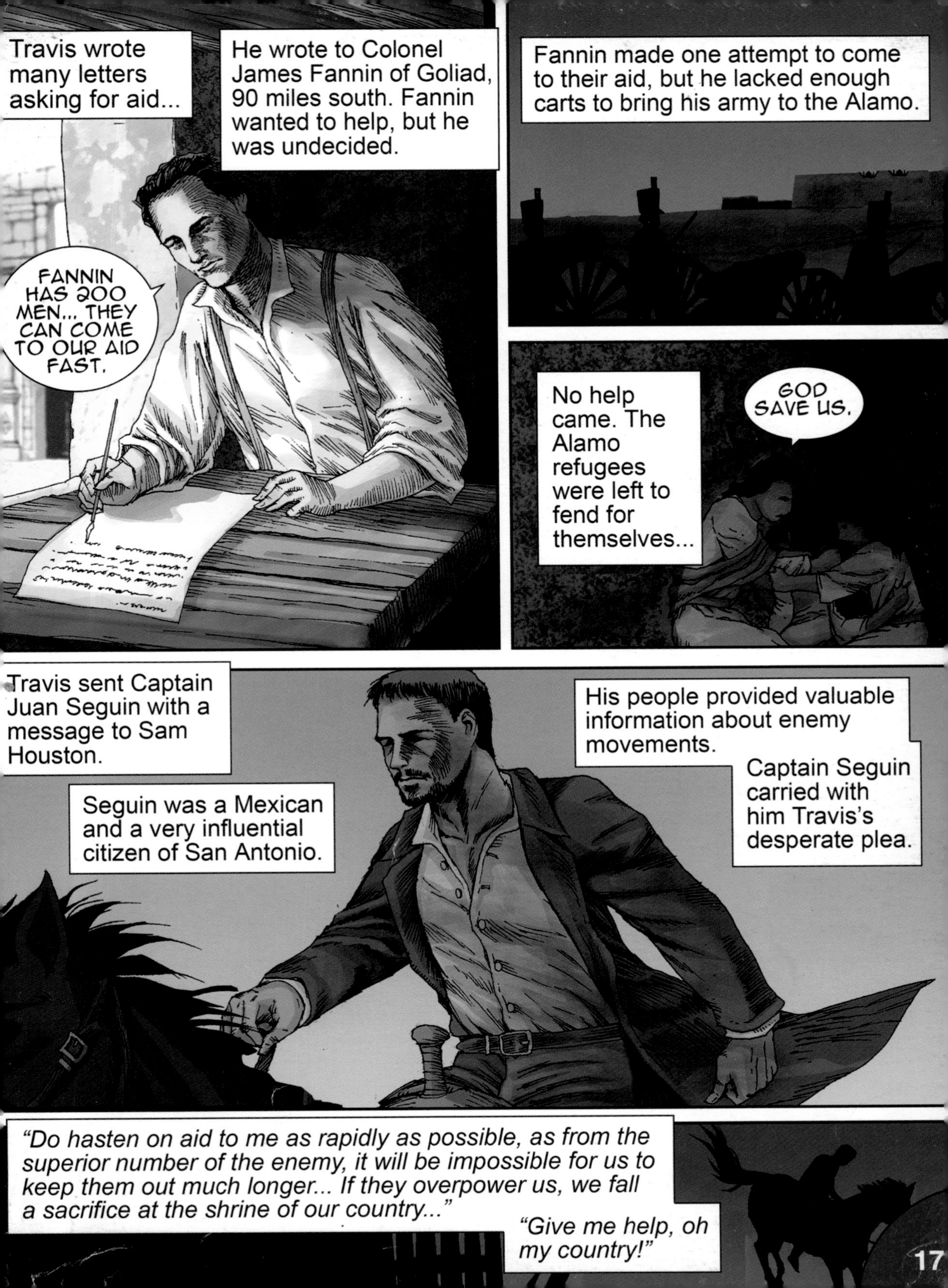
Travis wrote many letters asking for aid...
He wrote to Colonel James Fannin of Goliad, 90 miles south. Fannin wanted to help, but he was undecided.
FANNIN HAS 200 MEN... THEY CAN COME TO OUR AID FAST.
Fannin made one attempt to come to their aid, but he lacked enough carts to bring his army to the Alamo.
No help came. The Alamo refugees were left to fend for themselves...
GOD SAVE US.
Travis sent Captain Juan Seguin with a message to Sam Houston.
Seguin was a Mexican and a very influential citizen of San Antonio.
His people provided valuable information about enemy movements.
Captain Seguin carried with him Travis's desperate plea.
"Do hasten on aid to me as rapidly as possible, as from the superior number of the enemy, it will be impossible for us to keep them out much longer... If they overpower us, we fall a sacrifice at the shrine of our country..."
"Give me help, oh my country!"

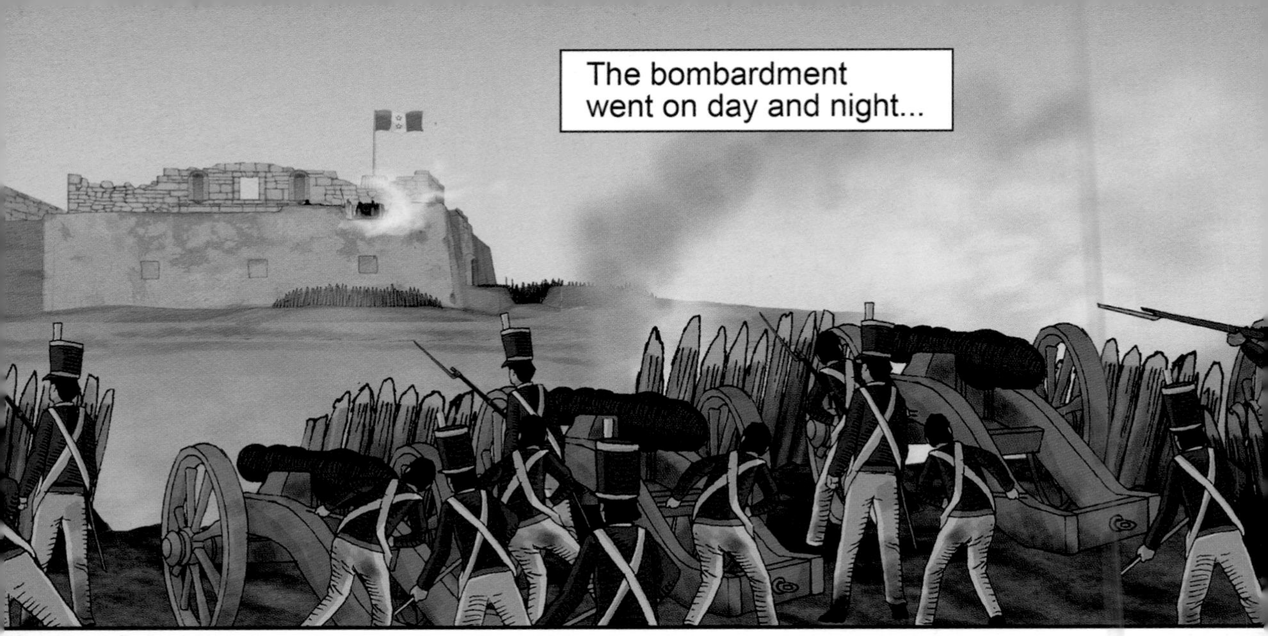
The bombardment went on day and night...

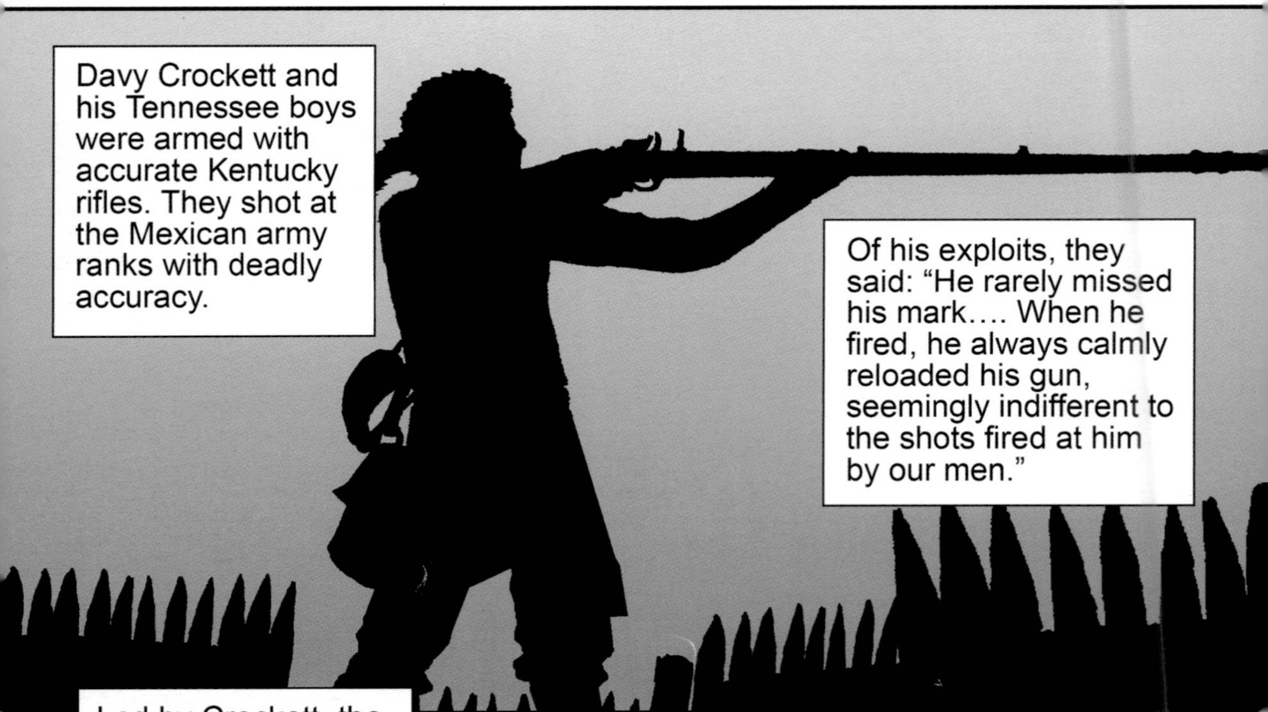
Davy Crockett and his Tennessee boys were armed with accurate Kentucky rifles. They shot at the Mexican army ranks with deadly accuracy.
Of his exploits, they said: "He rarely missed his mark…. When he fired, he always calmly reloaded his gun, seemingly indifferent to the shots fired at him by our men."

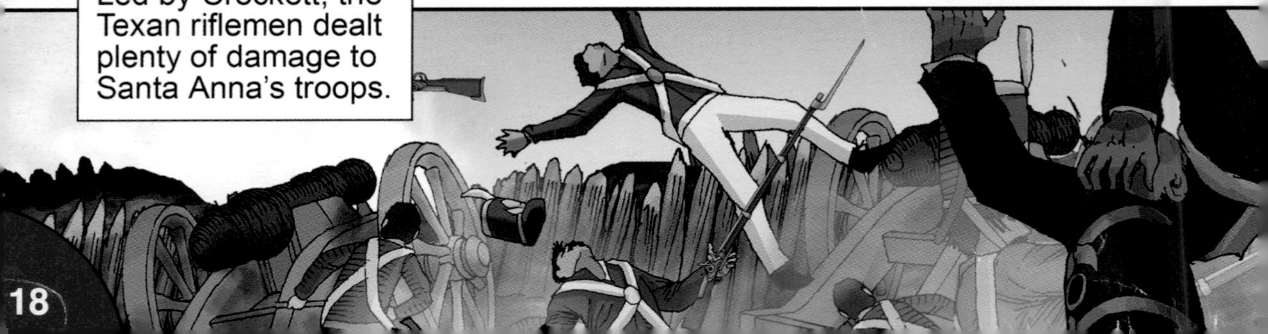
Led by Crockett, the Texan riflemen dealt plenty of damage to Santa Anna's troops.

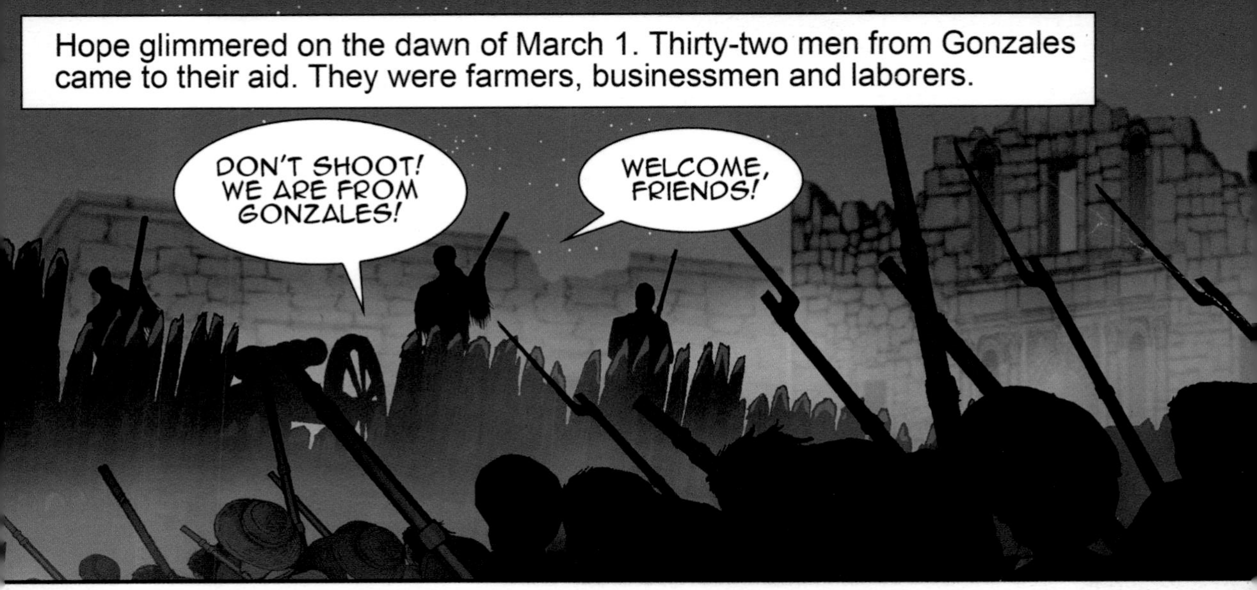
Hope glimmered on the dawn of March 1. Thirty-two men from Gonzales came to their aid. They were farmers, businessmen and laborers.
DON'T SHOOT! WE ARE FROM GONZALES!
WELCOME, FRIENDS!

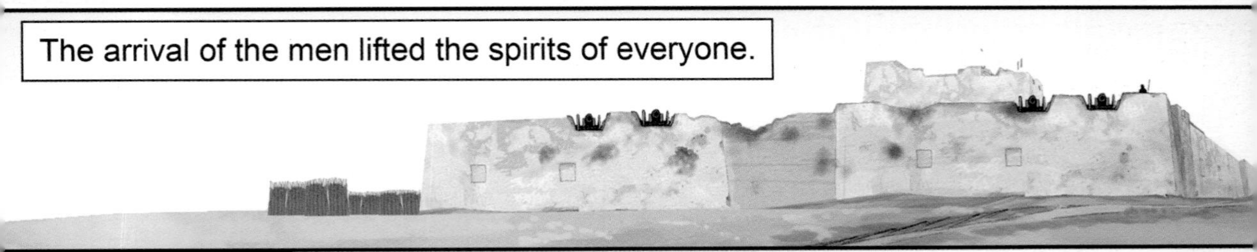
The arrival of the men lifted the spirits of everyone.

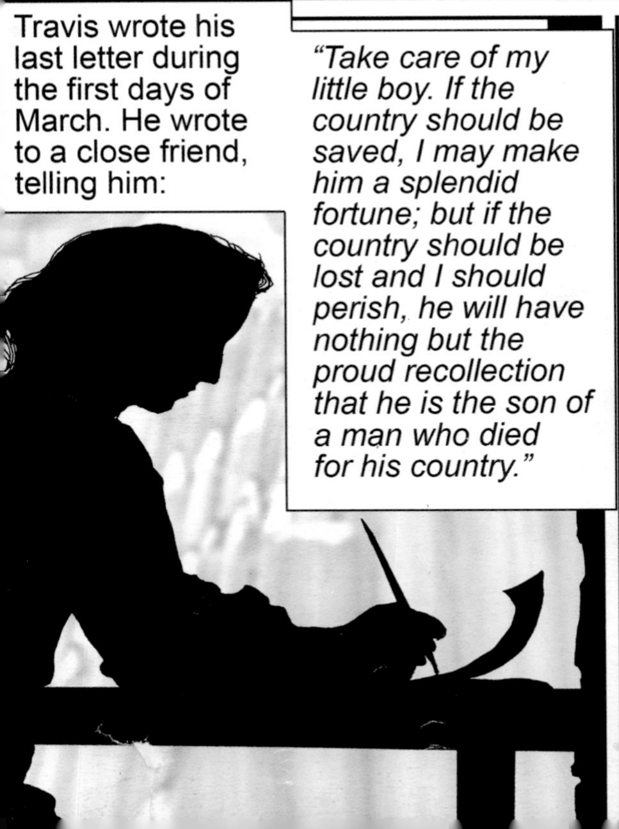
Travis wrote his last letter during the first days of March. He wrote to a close friend, telling him:
"Take care of my little boy. If the country should be saved, I may make him a splendid fortune; but if the country should be lost and I should perish, he will have nothing but the proud recollection that he is the son of a man who died for his country."

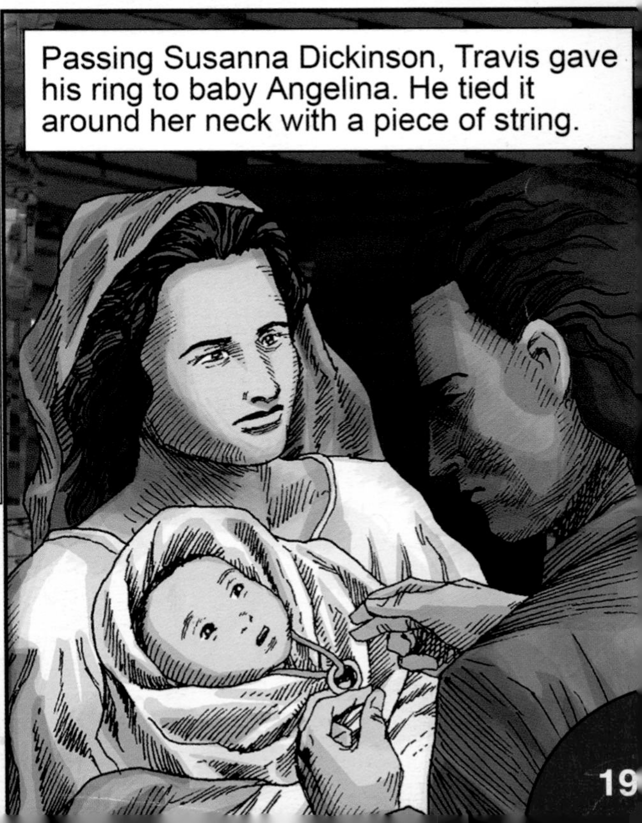
Passing Susanna Dickinson, Travis gave his ring to baby Angelina. He tied it around her neck with a piece of string.

Chapter 4 The Line in the Sand

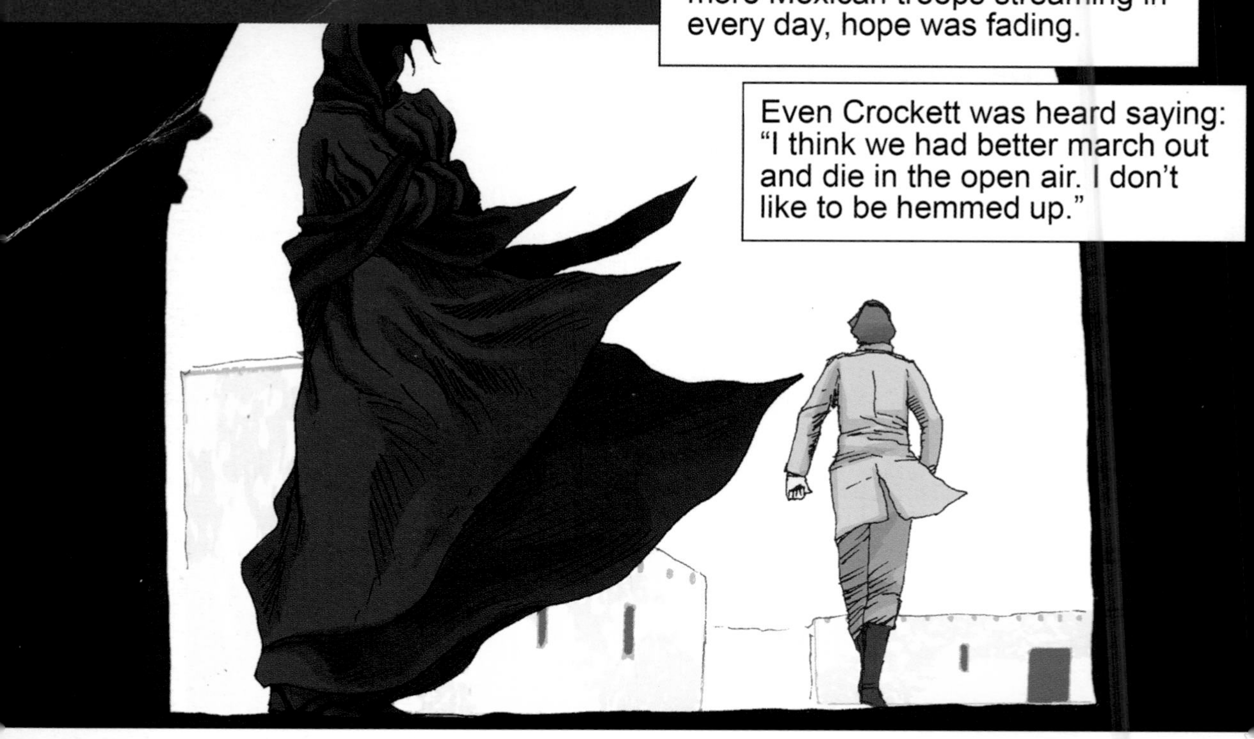
Things were looking dismal. With more Mexican troops streaming in every day, hope was fading.
Even Crockett was heard saying: "I think we had better march out and die in the open air. I don't like to be hemmed up."

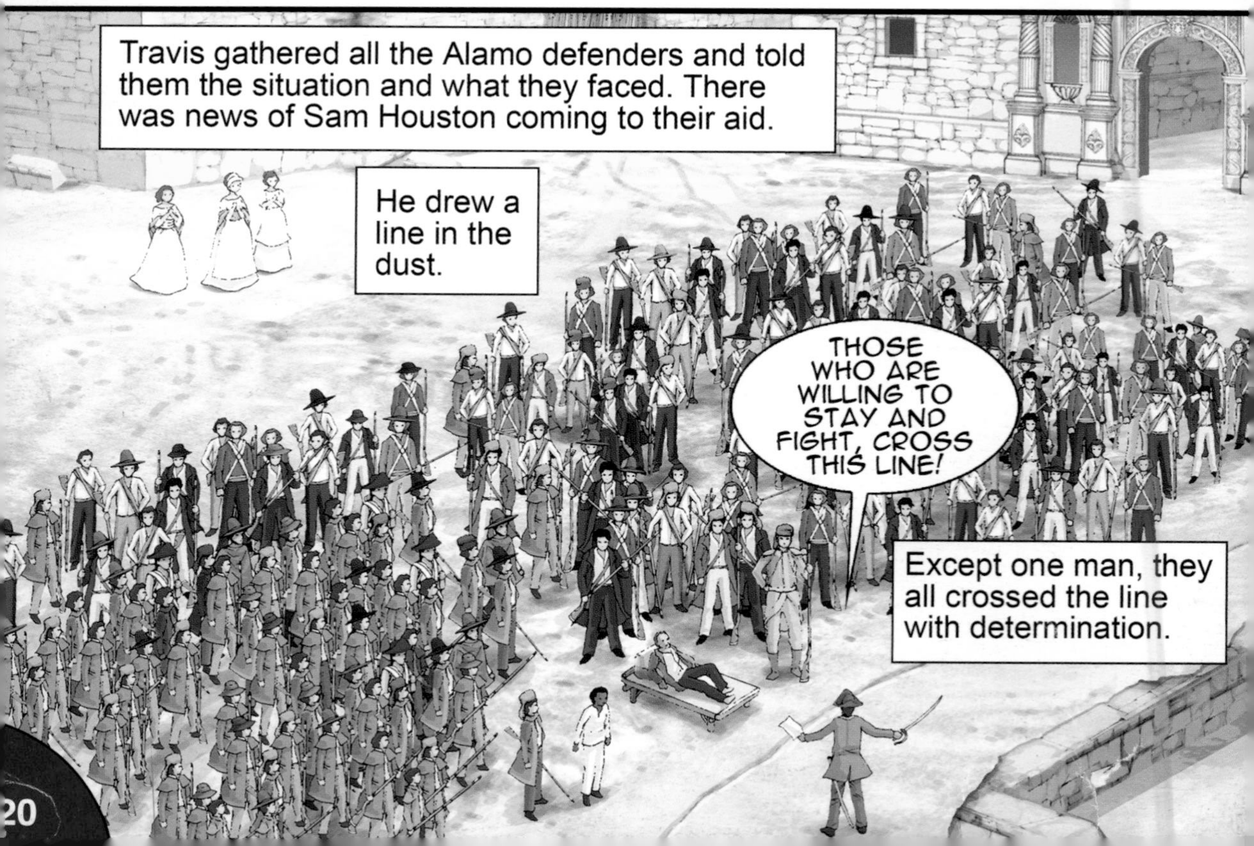
Travis gathered all the Alamo defenders and told them the situation and what they faced. There was news of Sam Houston coming to their aid.
He drew a line in the dust.
THOSE WHO ARE WILLING TO STAY AND FIGHT, CROSS THIS LINE!
Except one man, they all crossed the line with determination.

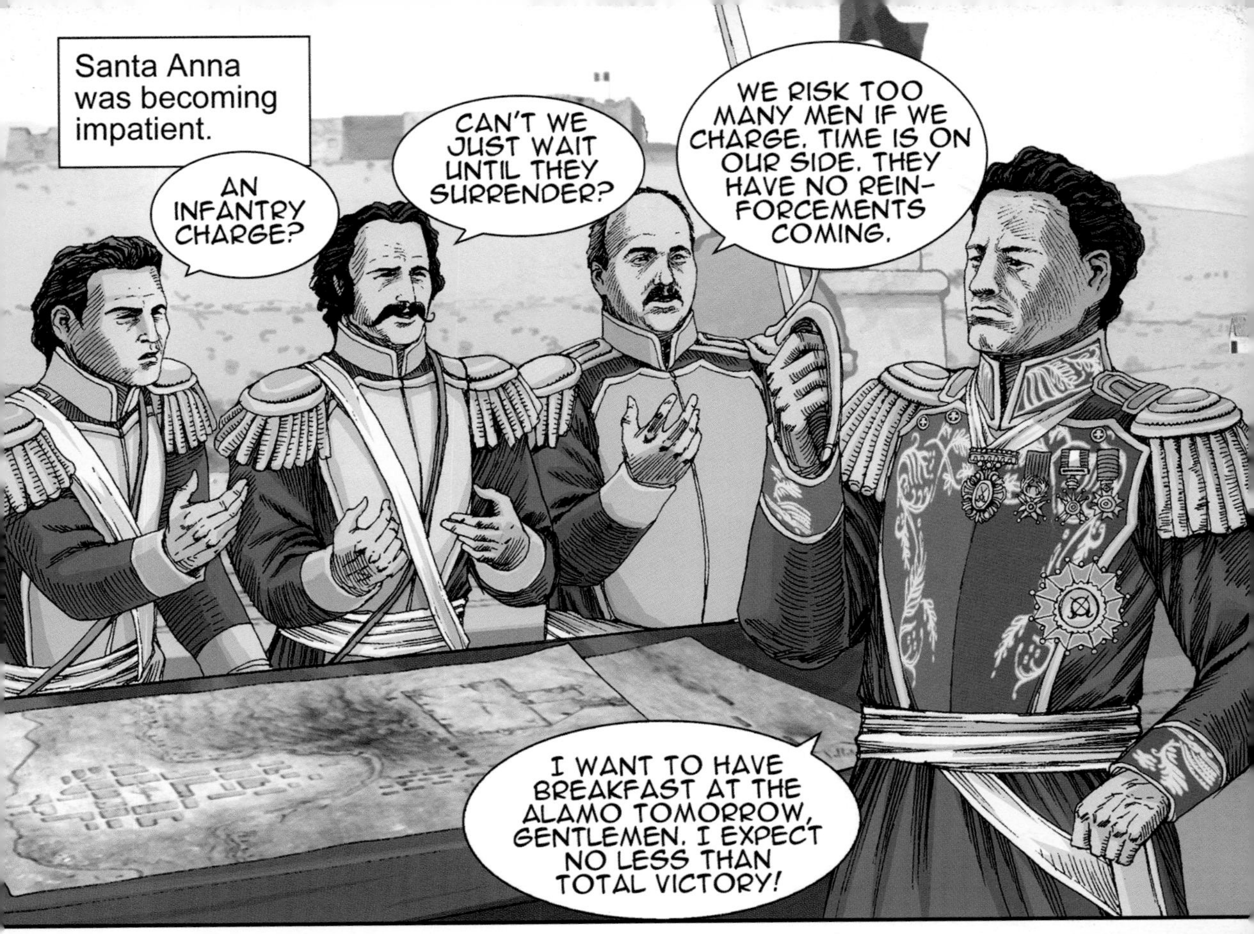
Santa Anna was becoming impatient.
AN INFANTRY CHARGE?
CAN'T WE JUST WAIT UNTIL THEY SURRENDER?
WE RISK TOO MANY MEN IF WE CHARGE. TIME IS ON OUR SIDE. THEY HAVE NO REIN-FORCEMENTS COMING.
I WANT TO HAVE BREAKFAST AT THE ALAMO TOMORROW, GENTLEMEN. I EXPECT NO LESS THAN TOTAL VICTORY!

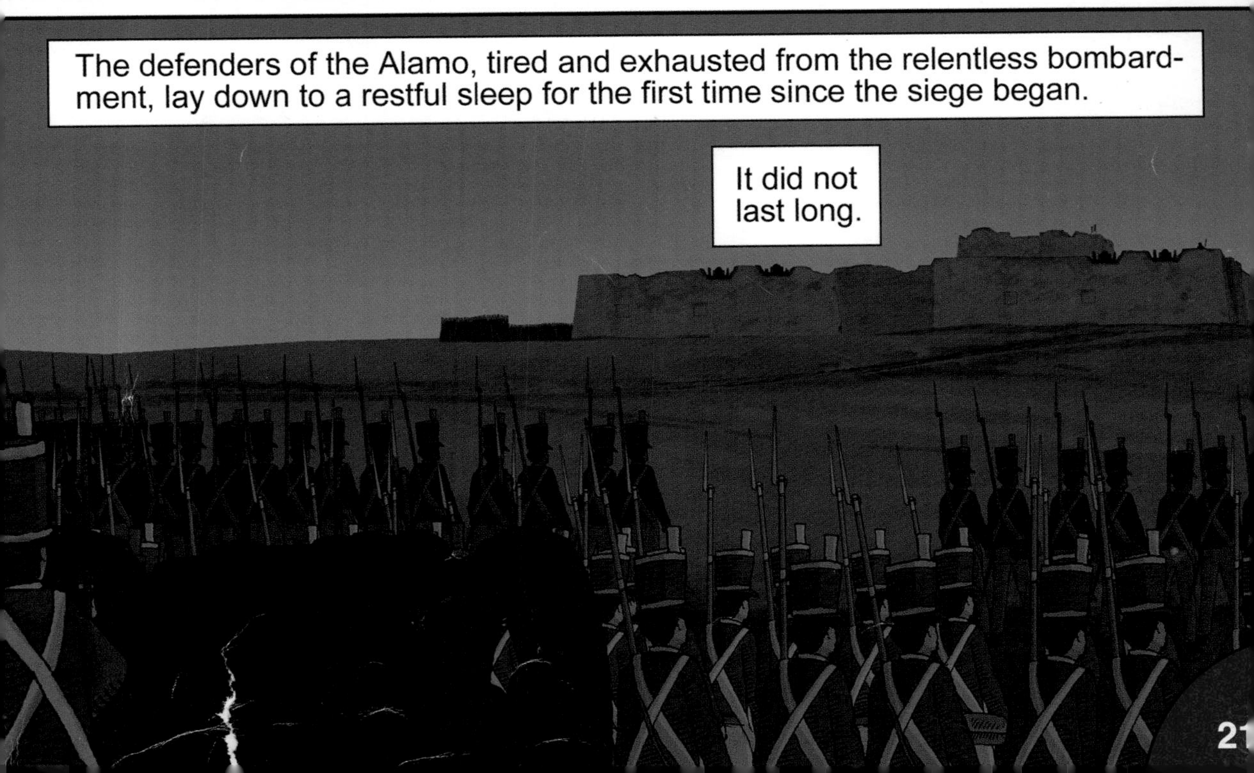
The defenders of the Alamo, tired and exhausted from the relentless bombard-ment, lay down to a restful sleep for the first time since the siege began.
It did not last long.

Chapter 5 The Battle of the Alamo

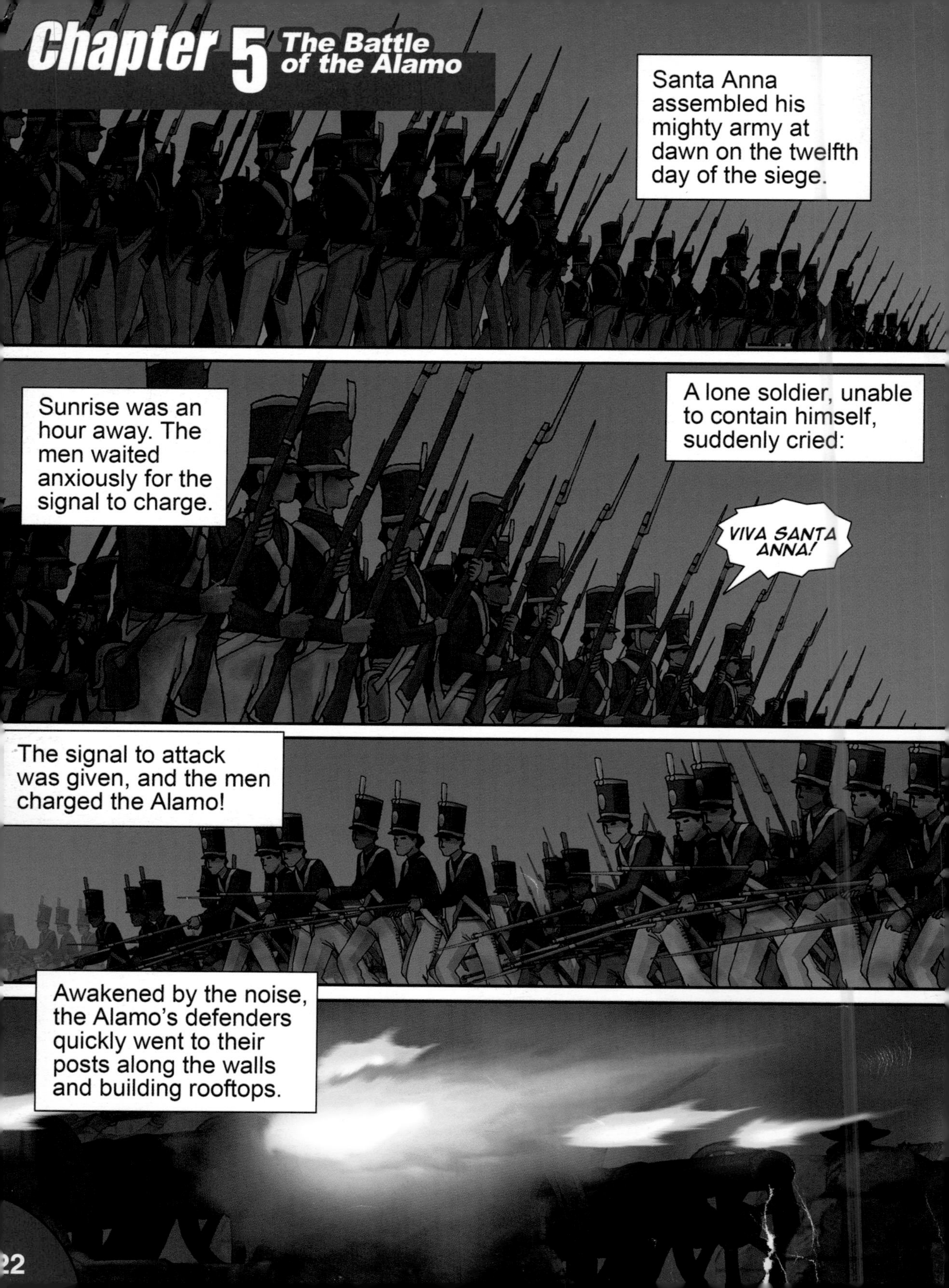
Santa Anna assembled his mighty army at dawn on the twelfth day of the siege.
Sunrise was an hour away. The men waited anxiously for the signal to charge.
A lone soldier, unable to contain himself, suddenly cried:
VIVA SANTA ANNA!
The signal to attack was given, and the men charged the Alamo!
Awakened by the noise, the Alamo's defenders quickly went to their posts along the walls and building rooftops.

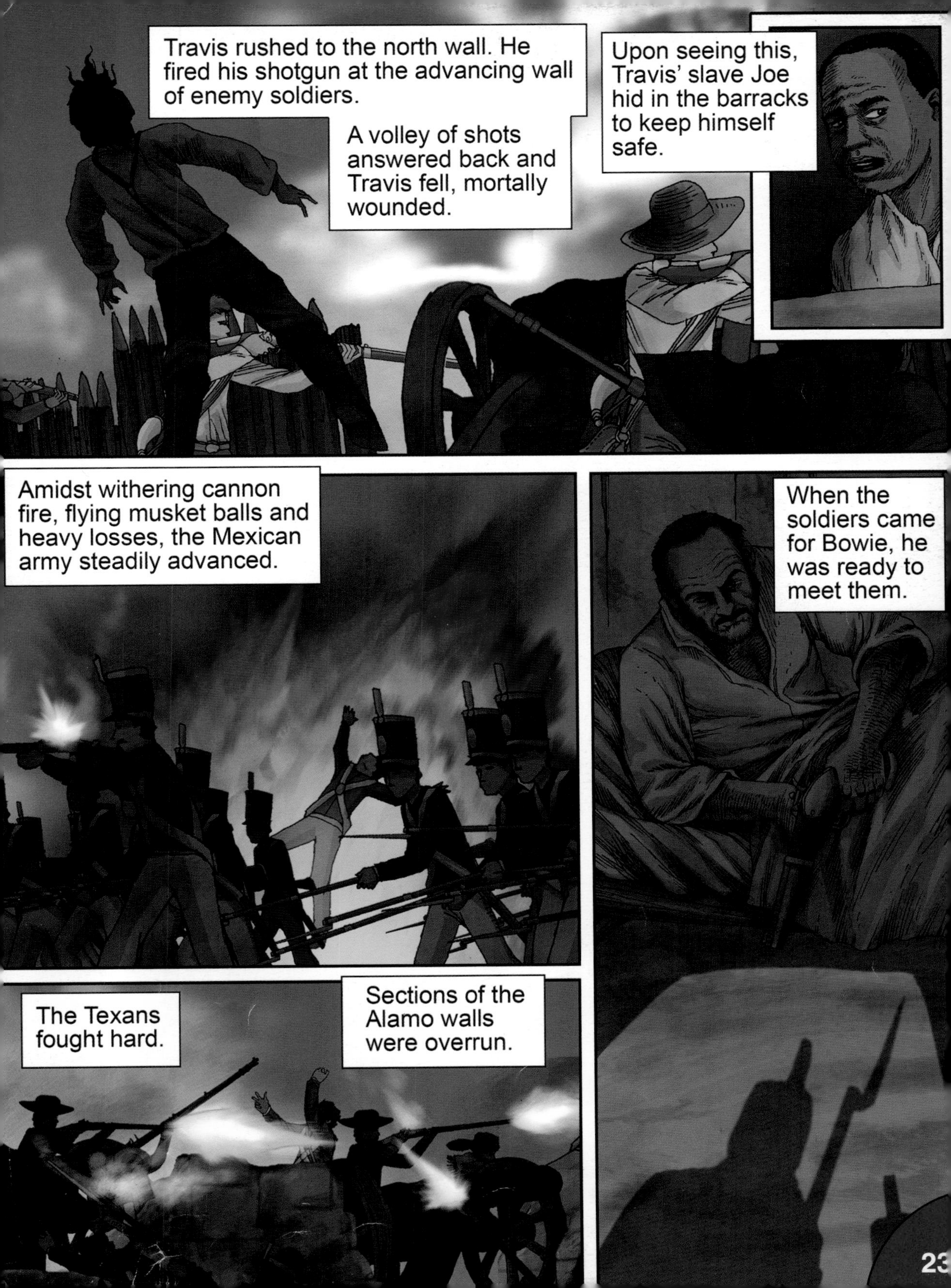

Travis rushed to the north wall. He fired his shotgun at the advancing wall of enemy soldiers.
A volley of shots answered back and Travis fell, mortally wounded.
Upon seeing this, Travis' slave Joe hid in the barracks to keep himself safe.
Amidst withering cannon fire, flying musket balls and heavy losses, the Mexican army steadily advanced.
When the soldiers came for Bowie, he was ready to meet them.
The Texans fought hard.
Sections of the Alamo walls were overrun.

Chapter 6 The Fall of the Alamo

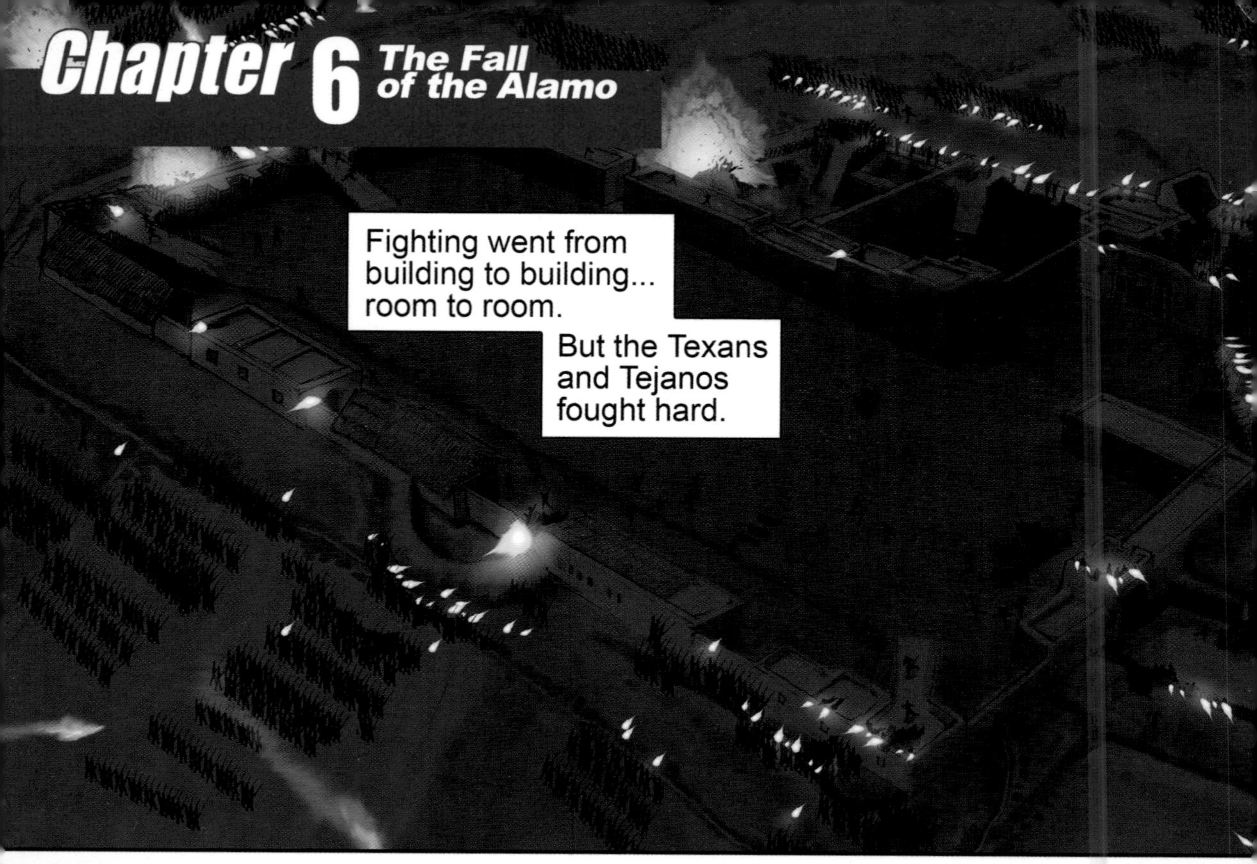
Fighting went from building to building... room to room.
But the Texans and Tejanos fought hard.

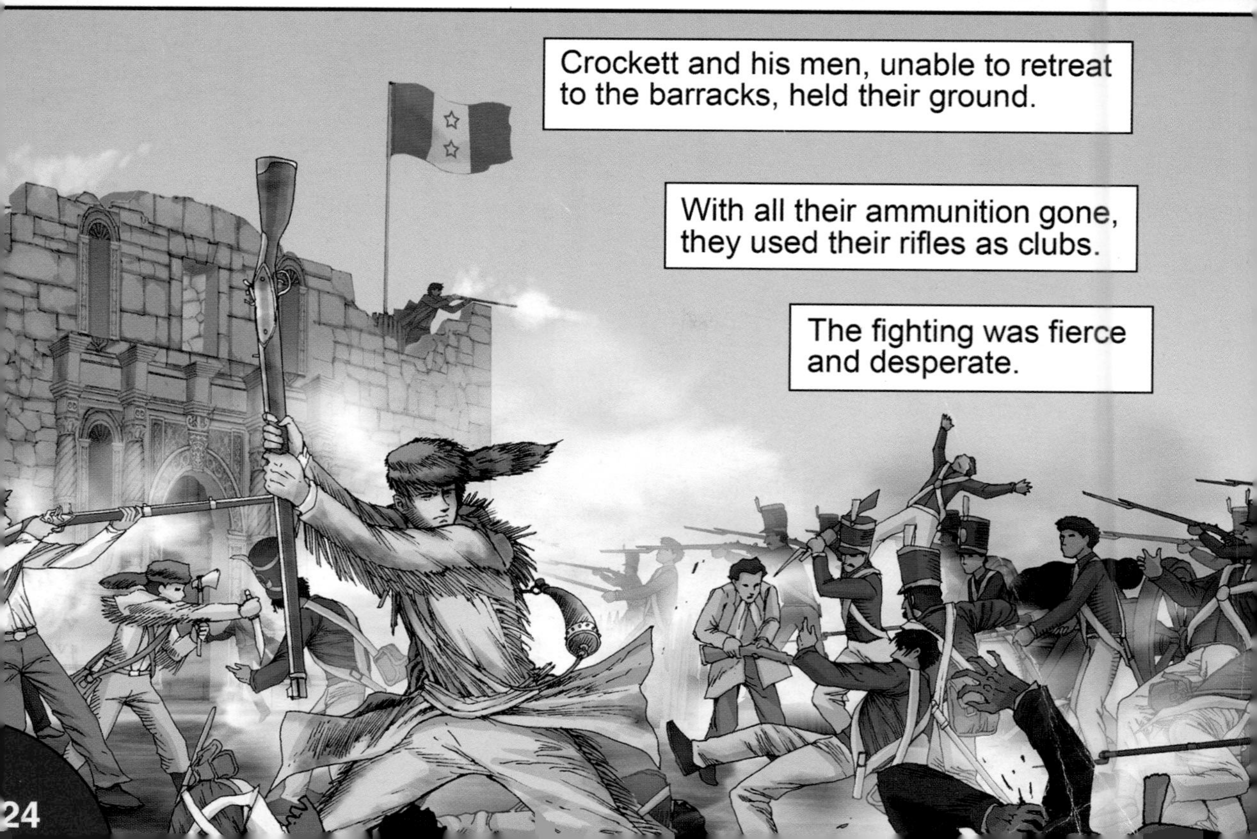
Crockett and his men, unable to retreat to the barracks, held their ground.
With all their ammunition gone, they used their rifles as clubs.
The fighting was fierce and desperate.

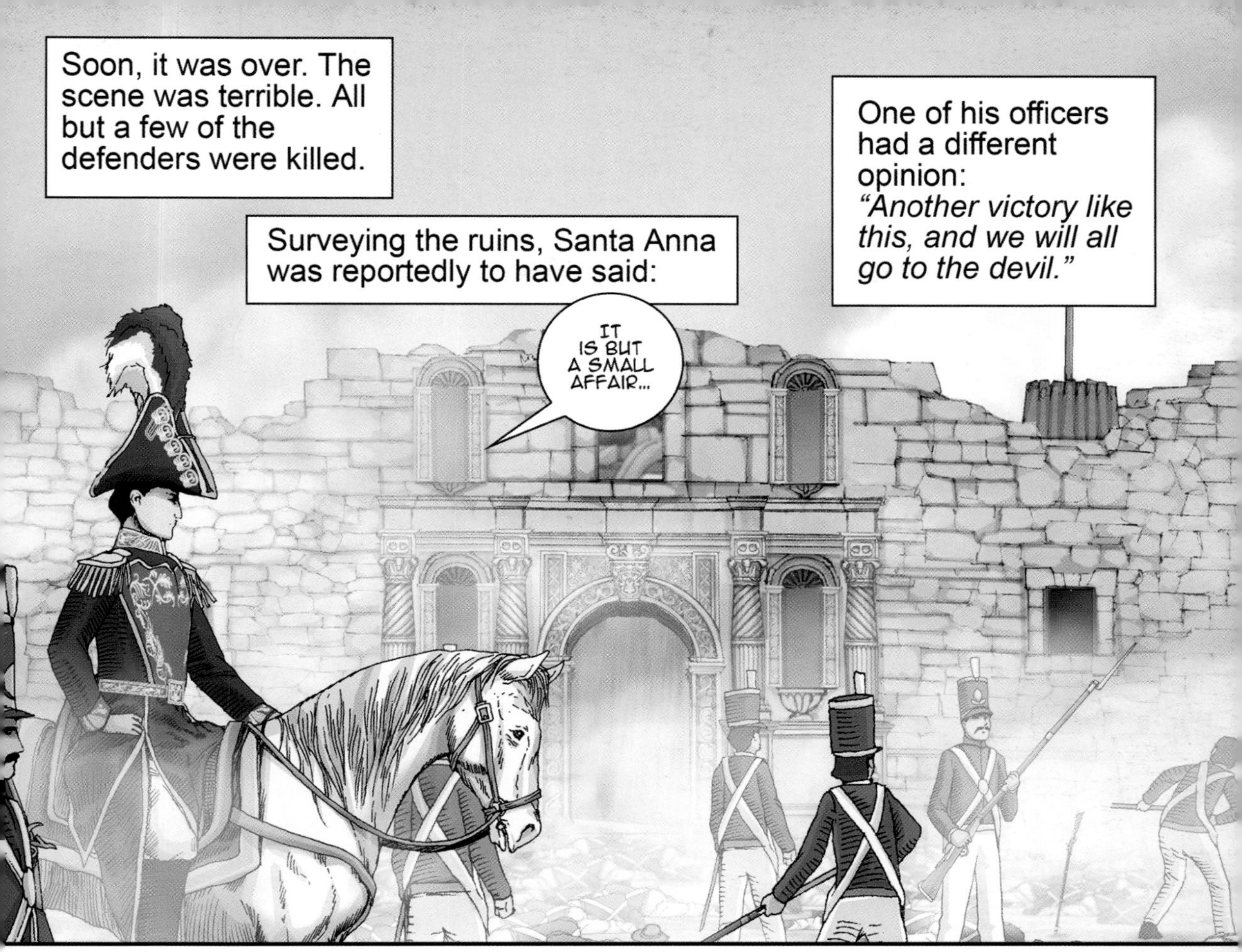
Soon, it was over. The scene was terrible. All but a few of the defenders were killed.
Surveying the ruins, Santa Anna was reportedly to have said:
IT IS BUT A SMALL AFFAIR...
One of his officers had a different opinion: *"Another victory like this, and we will all go to the devil."*

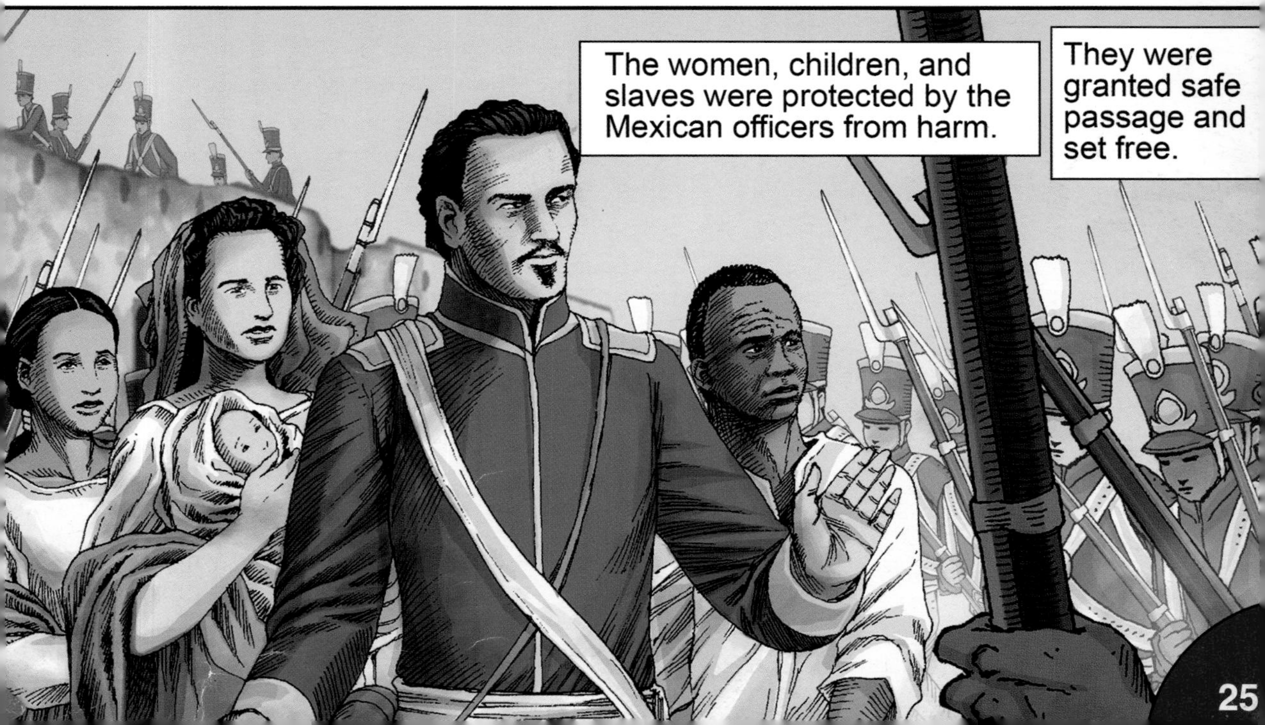
The women, children, and slaves were protected by the Mexican officers from harm.
They were granted safe passage and set free.

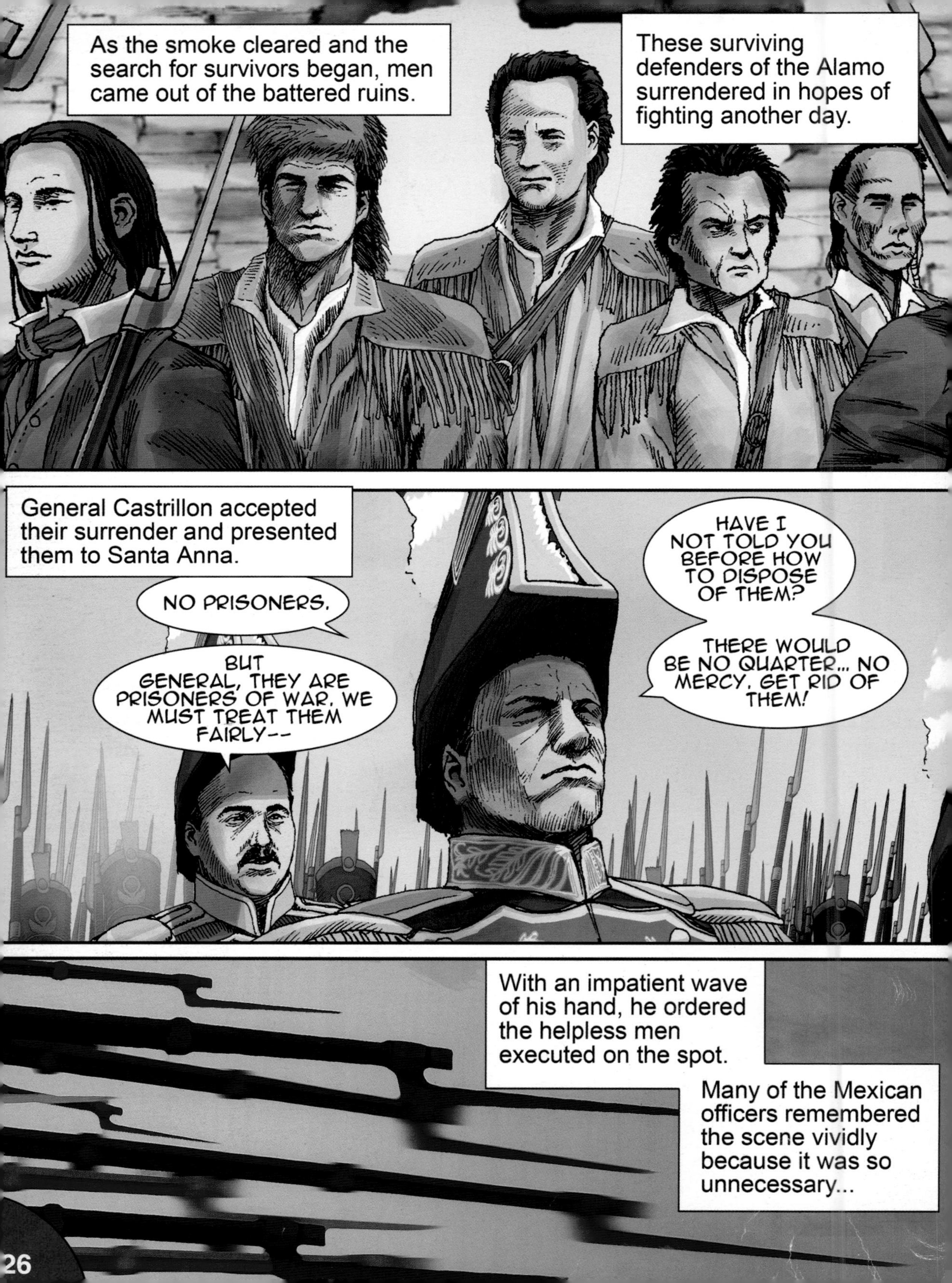
As the smoke cleared and the search for survivors began, men came out of the battered ruins.
These surviving defenders of the Alamo surrendered in hopes of fighting another day.
General Castrillon accepted their surrender and presented them to Santa Anna.
NO PRISONERS.
BUT GENERAL, THEY ARE PRISONERS OF WAR. WE MUST TREAT THEM FAIRLY--
HAVE I NOT TOLD YOU BEFORE HOW TO DISPOSE OF THEM?
THERE WOULD BE NO QUARTER... NO MERCY. GET RID OF THEM!
With an impatient wave of his hand, he ordered the helpless men executed on the spot.
Many of the Mexican officers remembered the scene vividly because it was so unnecessary...

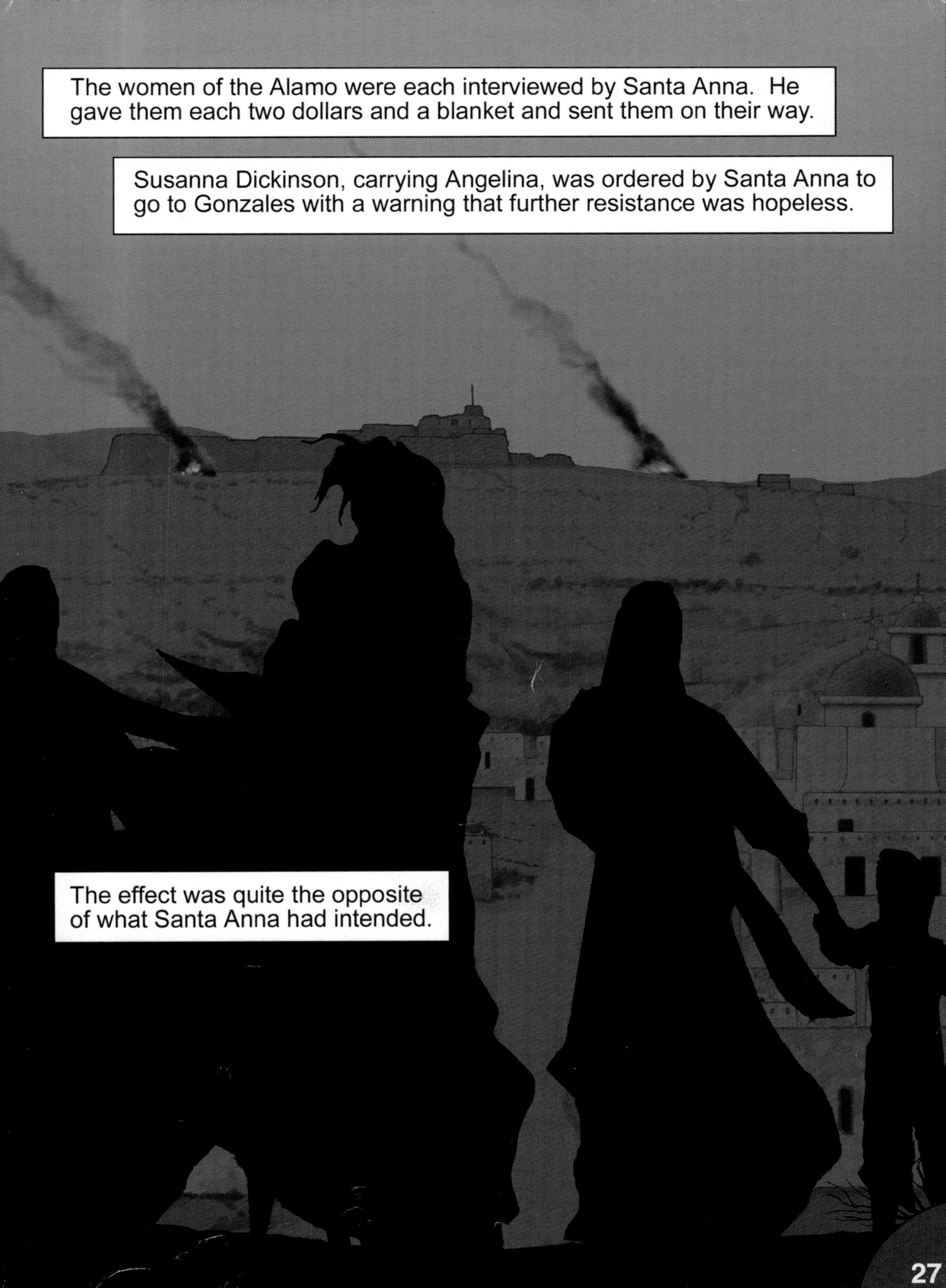
The women of the Alamo were each interviewed by Santa Anna. He gave them each two dollars and a blanket and sent them on their way.
Susanna Dickinson, carrying Angelina, was ordered by Santa Anna to go to Gonzales with a warning that further resistance was hopeless.
The effect was quite the opposite of what Santa Anna had intended.

Map of the Alamo

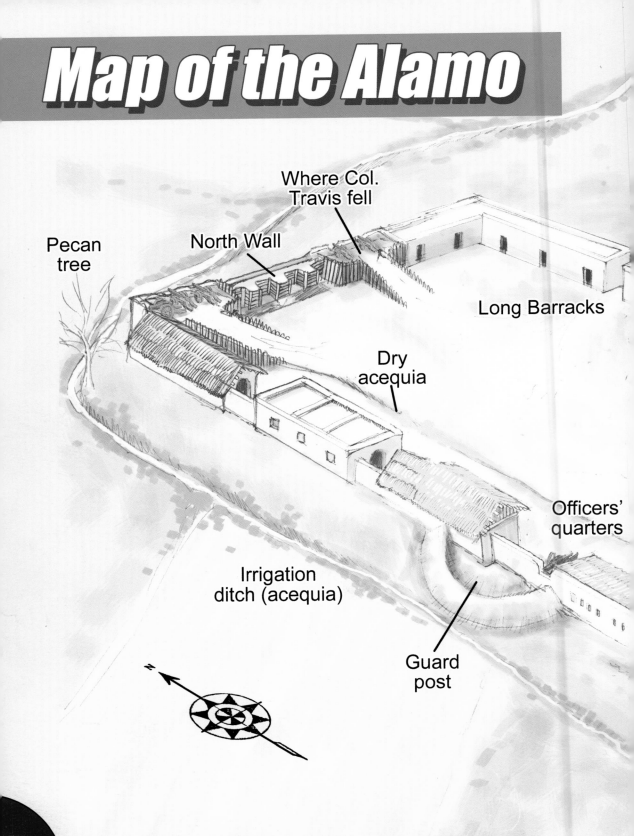

Where Col. Travis fell

Pecan tree

North Wall

Long Barracks

Dry acequia

Officers' quarters

Irrigation ditch (acequia)

Guard post

N

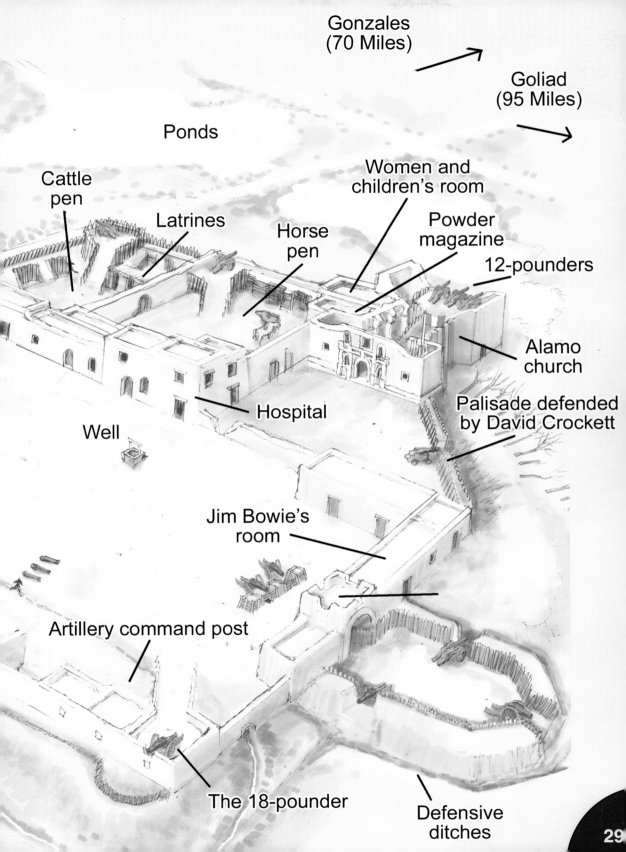

Gonzales
(70 Miles)

Goliad
(95 Miles)

Ponds

Cattle
pen

Latrines

Horse
pen

Women and
children's room

Powder
magazine

12-pounders

Alamo
church

Hospital

Well

Palisade defended
by David Crockett

Jim Bowie's
room

Artillery command post

The 18-pounder

Defensive
ditches

Timeline

1718 - Mission San Anton de Valero was founded.

1803 - The Mission was used as a military post. Soliders from the town of El Alamo inhabited the mission gaining the nickname, the Alamo.

1821 - Mexican independence was declared. Stephen F. Austin arrived in Texas with his first colonists.

1830 - The Mexican government restricted immigration into Texas from the north.

1832 - Colonists accused the Mexican government of many violations.

1835 - A skrimish occurred between Mexican troops and rebel settlers, rebels took control of the Alamo in December.

February 3, 1836 - William Barret Travis arrived with a small group of rebels.

February 8, 1836 - Former congressman David Crockett arrived with the Tennessee volunteers.

February 12, 1836 - Travis was named commander of the regular army; Jim Bowie led the volunteers.

February 23, 1836 - General Antonio López de Santa Anna arrived with his army in San Antonio. The Texan garrison retreated into the Alamo.

March 2, 1836 - Texas declared independence.

March 6, 1836 - The attack on the Alamo began before dawn. Estimates of Mexican losses are at least 600.

April 21, 1836 - The Texas army defeated the Mexican army at San Jacinto, Texas. General Santa Anna was captured. Texas independence was secured.

September 1836 - The Constitution of the Republic of Texas was established and Sam Houston was elected president of Texas.

Glossary

artillery - weapons, such as bows, slings, and catapults, that are used to send missiles.

captivate - to influence or hold attention with charm or irresistible appeal.

defiance - the act of resisting or fighting.

emplacement - a prepared position for weapons or military equipment.

gala - a gathering or celebration marking a special occasion.

palisade - a fence of strong, pointed stakes that protects against attack.

quarter - the act of showing mercy to the person or group one defeats. Giving quarter often means that the enemy is not killed.

Web Sites

To learn more about the Alamo, visit ABDO Publishing Company on the World Wide Web at **www.abdopublishing.com.** Web sites about the Alamo are featured on our Book Links page. These links are routinely monitored and updated to provide the most current information available.

Index

B

Bowie, James 5, 6, 13, 15, 23

C

Cassiano, Jose 4
Castrillon 26
Cos, Perfecto de 4
Crockett, David 5, 6, 13, 16, 18,
    20, 24

D

defenders 6, 12, 13, 16, 17, 18,
    21, 22, 23, 24, 25, 26
Dickinson, Almeron 10, 13
Dickinson, Susanna 10, 19, 20, 27

E

Esparza, George 11

F

Fannin, James 17

G

Goliad 17
Gonzales 19, 27

H

Houston, Sam 17, 20

M

Mayans 8
Mexican army 4, 7, 8, 9, 10, 13,
    15, 18, 20, 21, 22, 23, 25, 26
Mexico 4, 9, 17

N

Neill, James C. 5

S

San Antonio 7, 10, 17
San Fernando 13
Santa Anna, Antonio López de 9,
    13, 14, 15, 18, 21, 22, 25, 26,
    27
Seguin, Juan 17

T

Texas 4, 7, 23, 24
Travis, William Barret 5, 6, 13,
    16, 17, 19, 20, 23